The Piscataqua Gundalow
Workhorse for a Tidal Basin Empire

Gundalow under sail on the Squamscott River. Eugene Horne photo. PM.

The Piscataqua Gundalow
Workhorse for
A Tidal Basin Empire
by Richard E. Winslow III

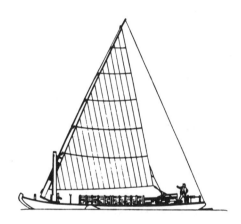

PORTSMOUTH MARINE SOCIETY
Publication Three

For my mother, Virginia, E. Winslow
who had the faith for my undertaking this book.

© 1983, 2002 by the Portsmouth Marine Society
Reprinted 2002
Printed in the United States of America

Design and produced by
    Peter E. Randall Publisher
    Box 4726, Portsmouth, NH 03802
    www.perpublisher.com

A publication of
Portsmouth Marine Society
Box 147, Portsmouth, NH 03802

Front cover photograph: Richard D. Conant
Rear cover photograph: Douglas Armsden

Library of Congress Cataloging in Publication Data
Winslow, Richard Elliott, III, 1934—
    The Piscataqua Gundalow
    (Publication / Portsmouth Marine Society; 3)
    Bibliography: p. Includes index.
    ISBN 0-915819-32-5 (PC)
1. Shipping—Piscataqua River (N.H. and Me.)—History. 2.
Gundalow—Piscataqua River Watershed (N.H. and Me.)—History. 3.
Adams, Edward Hamlin, 1860-1951. 4. Captain Edward H. Adams
(Boat). I. Title. II. Series: Publication (Portsmouth Marine Society); 3.
HE630.P57W56 1983
387.5'44'097426

83-2378

*The Portsmouth Marine Society is a non-profit, educational organization
established in 1982 to develop maritime historical research in the Piscataqua
River Basin of New Hampshire and Maine. Each illustrated, clothbound volume is complete with index, references, and bibliography. Selected titles are
available as paperback editions. As of May 2002, twenty-seven volumes have
been published in the series. For a list of available titles visit www.perpub-
lisher.com*

Contents

Introduction to the New Edition

WHEN THE GUNDALOW *Capt. Edward H. Adams* was launched from Prescott Park on June 13, 1982 she slid into the river stern first, sheered upriver a bit, and then delivered a solid thump to Babe Marconi's old pier. The collision knocked down a piling but didn't hurt the gundalow. Perhaps that was an omen of things to come.

As this book is being reprinted twenty years after that launch the vessel is in good shape; fresh planks and timbers have been fitted as necessary and she is oiled, caulked, and painted yearly. But institutionally the *Adams* must now begin a third life. She has been very successful educationally, but no one has yet devised a way to make her self-sufficient financially.

The vessel was built over three years and operated for its first thirteen years by the Piscataqua Gundalow Project. With a summer homeport at Prescott Park, the *Adams* traveled to most of the upriver and nearby alongshore communities in her first few years.

In 1988 the Board of Directors committed to an aggressive schedule of maintenance and activities. Vessel programs and revenues grew. I began my thirteen-year stint as skipper. But it became clear that a more active project required more sophisticated management. Meanwhile, Strawbery Banke Museum's President Denny O'Toole saw the possibilities of the gundalow for the museum's maritime history programs. In December 1994, after written safeguards for vessel care were negotiated, the gundalow and her programs became part of Strawbery Banke.

From 1995 through 2001 the *Adams* was active as a seasonal teaching platform for the museum with school field trips coming to Strawbery Banke in the spring, tourists and townspeople visiting Prescott Park in the summer, and a six-week visit to the Discovery Center at Sandy Point in Stratham each fall. She annually hosted 20,000 visitors. In 2001 management at Strawbery Banke decided that the *Adams*'s net cost was excessive and the museum decided to deaccession the gundalow.

A newly formed group called The Gundalow Company has now assumed responsibility for the vessel. We all hope they can continue the gundalow's important role in the community.

Michael Gowell
Kittery Point, July 2002

Acknowledgments

LIKE THE PISCATAQUA RIVER farmer who relied upon his neighbors' help in building and launching his gundalow, I have benefitted from the assistance of many. I have learned much from numerous people who have granted me interviews; and I hope I have accurately presented their views and observations. Without the infusion of their spirit, this book would merely be the bare bones of facts, dates, and numbers.

I am indebted to the ground breaking scholarship of my predecessors, D. Foster Taylor, William G. Saltonstall, Thomas E. Klewin, and William A. Baker.

For many contributions and courtesies, I thank the following institutions: The Piscataqua Gundalow Project; Portsmouth Marine Society; *Portsmouth Herald*; *Foster's Daily Democrat*; *New Hampshire Times*; Portsmouth Athenaeum; Woodman Institute, Dover; Old Berwick Historical Society, South Berwick, Maine; the historical societies of Portsmouth, Durham and Exeter; the public libraries of Portsmouth, Newmarket, Exeter, Rye, Dover and Rochester; Phillips Exeter Academy Library, Exeter; Dimond Library of the University of New Hampshire, Durham, especially the Media and Special Collections Departments; New Hampshire Historical Society, Concord; New Hampshire State Library, Concord; Maine Historical Society, Portland; Strawbery Banke, Portsmouth; Kittery Historical and Naval Museum, Kittery, Maine; Old Gaol Museum, York, Maine; John Hancock Warehouse Museum, York; Prescott Park, Portsmouth; Peabody Museum, Salem, Massachusetts; and Hart Museum of Massachusetts Institute of Technology, Cambridge, Massachusetts.

Frank C. Mevers, Archivist, Division of Records Management & Archives, Concord, searched the New Hampshire records and supplied superb manuscript reproductions. Peter E. Randall, publisher and friend, guided my efforts and handled many details concerning the book's design and photographs. Joseph G. Sawtelle supported my work, read my drafts, and arranged for other readers to check my manuscript.

I appreciate the efforts of the many photographers — Douglas Armsden, John Bardwell, Arnold Belcher, Eugene Horne, Bob LaPree, Peter Randall, and others—whose excellent pictures enhance this book. The Harvard University Press granted reproduction rights for the map of the Piscataqua Basin.

Ten people, in particular, have provided many kindnesses which have enriched this book.

Robert W. Corell, Director of the Marine Program at UNH and President of the Piscataqua Gundalow Project, brought me into the inner workings of this enterprise with interviews, contacts and unrestricted access to the Project's files. He also arranged for my passage aboard the *Heritage*, a vessel which escorted the gundalow replica on her maiden voyage from Portsmouth to Durham. Finally, Bob served as one of the readers of my completed manuscript and checked its accuracy.

Robert A. Whitehouse of Rollinsford, New Hampshire, an authority on gundalows, enthusiastically shared his vast knowledge on this subject. His valuable collection embraces two generations of historical research (Bob's father, the late Clyde Whitehouse, was a lifelong student of Piscataqua riverboats.) The elder Whitehouse preserved much material by jotting down on note cards the substance of his conversations with the old-timers back in the 1930s. Bob generously placed these unique materials in my hands.

Fred D. Crawford of Portland, Oregon, and Nancy A. Hunt of Braintree, Vermont, two longtime friends and professional writers, tackled the book's problems and aided my labor throughout with helpful comments on style and organization.

Joseph P. Copley, longtime Curator of the Portsmouth Athenaeum and expert on local history, made available that institution's resources for extensive research. Moreover, he performed yeoman service both in ferreting out obscure sources and in checking over and straightening out many difficult points.

Peggy Armitage, Irene Stivers, and Robert Eger, all closely associated with the work pertaining to the gundalow replica, *Captain Edward H. Adams*, read my drafts, corrected errors, and added important facts which clarified many matters to my original text. A member of the Project and former director of Strawbery Banke, Peggy Armitage contributed her detailed knowledge of these organizations. Irene Stivers, a hard-working member of the Project almost from its inception, provided much information about its activities. Robert Eger, the chief builder of the *Adams*, explained many technical aspects about the boat and assisted me in writing the captions for the construction photographs.

Richard and Virginia Winslow, my parents, encouraged my efforts and provided the essential support to enable me to write this book. They also cheerfully read my successive drafts and offered helpful suggestions.

To one and all, whether or not I have mentioned you by name, thank you for making *The Piscataqua Gundalow* a truly cooperative effort.

In the same connection, the Piscataqua Gundalow Project wishes to thank the many individuals and organizations involved with the entire *Captain Edward H. Adams* undertaking. Giving freely of their time, money, and materials, literally thousands of contributors carried the Project through to success. Among them are:

Spaulding-Potter Fund (Administered through UNH's Marine Program)	Wheelabrator Foundation
	Congoleum Corporation
	Dunfey Hotels
National Endowment for the Humanities	Montgomery Childs
	Mr. and Mrs. Michael Dingman
National Trust for Historic Preservation	Richard Gallant
	C. G. Rice
Fuller Foundation	B. Allen Rowland
Seacoast Savings Bank	Joseph G. Sawtelle, Jr.
Old Harbor Association	Mr. and Mrs. Cyrus B. Sweet III

I hope that both the book and the gundalow replica may add to the understanding of Piscataqua's illustrious history.

Little Harbor
Rye, New Hampshire
November 1981–January 1983.

Riding low in the water, a gundalow represented a common sight on the Piscataqua River for nearly 250 years. DAC.

Introduction

The Gundalow Legacy

GUNDALOWS were once the dominant cargo bearers of the Piscataqua River, moving supplies throughout the river basin of New Hampshire and Maine. For more than two hundred years, from colonial times through the nineteenth century, gundalows formed an indispensible link in a transportation network embracing over a thousand square miles of inland waters, from the river ports to Portsmouth on the seacoast. During their heyday, more than two thousand were built in this region. Without the Piscataqua gundalow, the development and growth of the entire basin would have been severely hampered. The gundalow was a symbol of its age, just as the railroad, the motor truck, and the jet airplane represent later ones. Today the gundalow is gone, a victim of technological displacement. But at its zenith, this specialized vessel was superior to any other carrier.[1]

Despite the contributions of the gundalow, which evolved from a crude barge with a square sail to a sophisticated craft with a deck, rudder, and triangular sail, its full story remains to be told. The early gundalow captains were usually farmers who built their own craft during long winters. Frequently unlettered, these men seldom kept records, or if they did, their ledgers and commercial papers were rarely preserved. Early historians and journalists found more glamour and excitement — and reached more readers — in recording the exploits of clippers and whalers. "The gundalow was so commonplace," William Dennett, a local maritime historian, notes, "that no particular attention was paid to it; it was as common as a truck passing by today."[2]

A few scholarly articles, some newspaper articles, and occasional captions below photographs in regional travel books represent the entire printed record of the gundalow. A few models, frequently constructed from the boards of derelict gundalows, repose in museums. This study fills a long-standing historical gap by bringing together much scattered material. It tries to go beyond the mere collection, assemblage, and evaluation of facts. It is concerned as well with the Yankee spirit and the ability to improvise.

The gundalow represents a monument to the zeal of New England pioneers who faced a problem. To rely upon the king and Parliament in London or upon the later American government, remote in either case, was senseless and impractical. As Thomas Dudley, a Portsmouth lawyer and Piscataqua Gundalow Project officer, observes,

> The gundalow represents something peculiar to this area. The local people back in those times didn't turn to Washington and the government. They solved their transportation problem by themselves and were not dependent upon outside help.[3]

Long before Benjamin Franklin and Eli Whitney appeared on the scene, Yankee pioneers and their descendants puttered around in a country workshop or barn, experimented, failed, and tried again. We do not know the name of the builder of the first Piscataqua gundalow. Whether this person was literate, a church-goer, or a local village official is immaterial. What is important is that he had an idea (or cribbed it unashamedly from his Old World background), persevered to work out the kinks, and launched the gundalow.

The legacy left by the gundalowmen has been recognized by a group of present-day Piscataqua citizens. By building a replica of this craft, the Piscataqua Gundalow Project officers and members are fostering a spirit of historical inquiry for students and others who will visit this floating classroom and exhibit. Yankee interest in technology, exemplified by the replica, is an inherited and ingrained characteristic of this area. The gundalow project complements other efforts to preserve the past of this historic region.

The Broad Impact of the Gundalow

The gundalow affected the entire spectrum of the economic, military, and cultural history of the Piscataqua River basin. In economic terms, the importance of the gundalow is undisputed. Called a "drowned valley,"

"Great Bay Gundalow" (1879), oil painting by H. H. Hallett. GB.

the Piscataqua River, with its half-dozen tributaries and Little and Great Bays, serves as a vital artery connecting all its inland points to the sea. The gundalows took advantage of both the flood and ebb tides for fast runs. They typically carried wood, marsh grass and bricks to Portsmouth, and returned inland with manufactured goods and coal.

The military use of the gundalow, an all-purpose craft which could haul anything and go anywhere, is amply documented in the New Hampshire archives for the colonial wars and the Revolution. The varied accounts of the two patriot raids on Fort William and Mary at New Castle, at the entrance of Portsmouth harbor, dispute most points: How many men were involved? How much powder was seized from the British magazines? Where was it stored? Despite the continuing controversy, one point remains uncontested. Every authority concurs that gundalows were the craft used to carry the raiders to the fort, and then to transport the powder back to the bay villages.

Culturally, the gundalow is represented in painting, photography, fiction, and poetry. In their panoramic depictions of harbor and river scenes, the landscape painters included the gundalow. Later, photographers, in their grainy shots of mills and docks, caught the gundalow with the lens. Many examples of this art are reproduced in this book. For authenticity and local color, poets and novelists also described gundalows.

Other Centers of Gundalow Activity

The gundalow is not unique to the Piscataqua area, but nowhere in North America, perhaps even in the world, did the gundalow play such a pre-eminent role in a local economy. In other locales, the gundalow was merely a secondary component of the transportation network. As Charles E. Clark, American historian and specialist on early New England, observes,

> It is true that other communities had what they called gundalows, whether they were or not. Perhaps they hired them for the day to transport hay, but they were never a major part of the transportation network as they were here on the Piscataqua. The gundalows were really the key method of transportation in the Piscataqua River area.[4]

Other places near and far used (and in some cases still use) the Piscataqua type gundalow.

After their success in the Piscataqua basin, gundalows soon appeared on Lake Winnipesaukee in central New Hampshire. They carried goods between Alton Bay, Meredith and other lake ports, and were noted for their safety. There is no record of anyone being lost in an accident. The doom of these lake gundalows was sealed with the invention of the "horseboat," an odd combination of scow, team, and treadmill, with the horses walking the treads to turn the side-wheels. These horseboats, first built in 1837–1838, soon drove the gundalows out of business.[5]

In Maine, especially on the Kennebec River, the gundalows flourished during colonial times and continued until the late nineteenth century. In his definitive study of maritime activity in the Kennebec region, the late William A. Baker mentions "these ubiquitous craft" all along the New England seaboard. Baker states that the hulls of the Kennebec version "remained square as long as employed on that river," differing from the mature Piscataqua model.[6] The port of Casco Bay further south at Falmouth (now Portland) prospered with the West Indian trade during the 1700s. Carrying various cargoes, gundalows plied up and down the Presumpscot River and its branches and at Back Cove. On the Mousam River, the port of Kennebunk was crowded with gundalows after the Revolution. The York River also saw much gundalow activity.[7]

The Merrimack River basin of Massachusetts ranked perhaps

Model of Merrimack River gundalow built by Joseph Lowe, West Newbury, Massachusetts in 1862, and displayed at the Peabody Museum. A representation of the gundalow's intermediate stage with bow and stern decks and square sail. Note the sweeps carried for propulsion. PM.

second to the Piscataqua in volume of gundalow traffic. In the stretch between Haverhill and Newburyport gundalows were once a familiar sight on the river and nearby salt marshes. In 1862, in the planning stage of building his own gundalow, Joseph Lowe of West Newbury constructed a model. Today Lowe's model is on display at the Peabody Museum in Salem. In their prime, gundalows were employed to load and unload vessels in Newburyport harbor. Ironically, they hastened their own demise by assisting in the construction of wharves and bridges, including the Eastern Railroad bridge built across the Merrimack in 1840.[8]

Along the North River to the south of Boston, the settlers needed to harvest the marsh grass as feed for their cattle and horses. In the towns of Scituate and Marshfield, gundalows carried the cut hay upland where it could be carted away.[9]

Merrimack River gundalows collecting stacks of marsh hay cut along the estuary. Watercolor by H. H. Hallett. PM.

On Lake Champlain and the St. Lawrence River during the Revolutionary War, gundalows fought under both the American and British flags. Despite the same name, the man-of-war gundalow bore no relation, beyond its flat bottom, to the Piscataqua type. These military gundalows were much more complex in their design and rigging, and carried, depending upon their size, from two to ten guns. Benedict Arnold is said to be responsible for the general design of the gundalows and galleys on Lake Champlain.[10] On the West Coast of the United States, some of the fishing boats in San Francisco Bay closely resemble the Piscataqua gundalow style.

Elsewhere, in waters around the globe, vessels with a lateen sail have been favorites since early times. On the Nile River in Egypt feluccas have "moved on a whisper of the wind since the days of the pharaohs." To this day tourists can rent feluccas for $5.00 an hour for pleasure sailing.[11]

Long before the fall of the Roman Empire, vessels with similar designs and lateen or triangular sails were heavily used in the Mediterranean. (The word "lateen" derives from the word "Latin.")

Arab dhows still sail in Mid-Eastern waters and on the east coast of Africa. Even there the lateen sail is giving way to the diesel engine as a source of power. It is believed that Sinbad the Sailor's ship must have been a dhow.[12]

This hardy flat bottomed vessel, like the legendary phoenix, rises periodically from its ashes despite rumors of its extinction. Whether called a gundalow, felucca, or dhow, it has been invented, re-invented, copied, changed and modified to local needs for thousands of years. Other types of craft come and go, but the gundalow endures, appearing in the world wherever cheap water transportation is required. The Piscataqua gundalow is thus a descendant of the earliest boats in recorded history.

Researching the Gundalow

This book focuses on the Piscataqua gundalow. The first chapter deals with the gundalow's history. The second concerns Captain Edward H. Adams (1860 – 1951), the last of the gundalow builders and skippers. The final chapter describes the recent construction of the modern gundalow, *Captain Edward H. Adams*, at Strawbery Banke. A saga in its own right, the building of this gundalow under the auspices of the Piscataqua Gundalow Project begins with searching for the right trees in the forests and ends with sailing the gundalow to Durham for the 250th anniversary of the founding of that town. Wherever practical, the shipwrights used traditional materials, techniques and tools to create as authentic a replica as possible. The only major difference is the present cost, enough to make New Hampshire colonists revolt a second time.

Written sources on the gundalow are meager. Not until 1937 did the first study of the gundalow appear, written by D. Foster Taylor under the sponsorship of the Works Progress Administration. His thirty-nine page typescript was ultimately published (with some deletions) as two articles in the *American Neptune* in 1942. In 1941, William G. Saltonstall produced his *Ports of Piscataqua*, which contains an excellent chapter on the gundalow. Both writers sought out and interviewed Captain Adams, who was then building his last gundalow, *Driftwood*, on Great Bay. Subsequent printed information derives from these two studies.

The role of Captain Adams is documented in periodical literature and in the Adams Family Papers. Local reporters, realizing that the gundalow era was almost over and that Adams was the last remaining link to those times, made the pilgrimage to see him. Fortunately, when the research for this book was beginning, the Adams Family Papers were opened at the Special Collections Department, Dimond Library, the University of New Hampshire, Durham. For recollections about the Captain and his son, Cass, now both deceased for more than twenty years, I have talked with their former neighbors.

Interviews have been indispensable to describe the construction of the *Captain Edward H. Adams*. The shipwrights, blacksmiths, and others directly involved with the Piscataqua Gundalow Project have told me of their day-to-day battle with cumbersome logs and unruly adzes at the Strawbery Banke boatyard. Some of this ordeal is preserved on film shot by the UNH Educational TV station, Channel 11. The files of the Piscataqua Gundalow Project, housed at the Marine Program Building at the University of New Hampshire, contain much essential material.

Each gundalow was unique, built without blueprints, and spelled as well with many variants. I have retained the variant spellings in my quotations. Like the spellings, the very nature of this type of history is often inexact and spotty. Modern military, diplomatic, and political history is blessed with complete archives, newspaper files, and voluminous memoirs of the principals involved. The availability of quantities of information makes the historian's work comparatively easy; only interpretation remains a problem.

The Piscataqua gundalow's history, on the other hand, relies on scattered and incomplete records, as well as on the memory of people who may have forgotten an exact date or a complete name. The oral tradition, however, remains the only available resource to fill the gaps in the written record. While talking with many old-timers, I moved back in time with them as they described the thrilling days of the gundalows and their captains. I have tried to capture the spirit of their words, split-second illuminations into the darkness of the past.

The Spirit of the Gundalow

Many New England writers have presented the legends of the gundalow era in their poems, essays, and novels. The spirit of the gundalow survives in writings about the Piscataqua basin and other nearby New England rivers.

John Greenleaf Whittier, a native of Haverhill, Massachusetts, saw many gundalows on the Merrimack River. In his masterpiece,

"Snow-bound" (1866), Whittier describes lying

> Stretched idly on the salted hay
> Adrift along the winding shores,
> When favoring breezes deigned to blow
> The square sail of the gundelow
> And idle lay the useless oars.[13]

Again in "The Countess" (1863), Whittier writes of the Merrimack:

> The river's steel-blue crescent curves
> To meet, in ebb and flow,
> The single broken wharf that serves
> For sloop and gundelow.[14]

In her *Country By-Ways* (1881), Sarah Orne Jewett, a lifelong resident of the gundalow port of South Berwick, Maine, observes,

> When you catch sight of a tall lateen sail, and a strange, clumsy craft that looks heavy and low in the water, you will like to know that its ancestor was copied from a Nile boat, from which a sensible old sea-captain took a lesson in ship-building many years ago. The sail is capitally fitted to catch the uncertain wind, which is apt to come in flaws and gusts between the high, irregular banks of the river; and the boat is called a gundalow, but sometimes spelled gondola. One sees them often on the Merrimac and on the Piscataqua and its branches...[15]

In 1923, Albertus T. Dudley, a resident of Exeter and one-time teacher at Phillips Exeter Academy, published a juvenile novel, *The King's Powder* (1923), based on the 1774 Fort William and Mary raid. He mentions the use of gundalows in this fictional account.[16]

Novelist Kenneth Roberts, noted for his absorbing plots and painstaking historical research, recalls the gundalow. His great work, *Northwest Passage* (1936) presents the hero, Langdon Towne, musing on about

> the broad reaches of the Piscataqua, running down toward Portsmouth; the squat gundelos with lateen sails that came to the landing with their loads of goods for the back country.[17]

A few pages later, Towne navigates his "gundelo" across the Piscataqua

"Church Point" Portsmouth, New Hampshire (1883), watercolor by Childe Hassam (1859–1935). A Massachusetts-born artist and friend of Celia Thaxter, Hassam was a frequent visitor to Appledore Island and seacoast New Hampshire during the 1880s and 1890s. GB.

from Kittery, Maine, to Portsmouth to call on his lady love in that town.

In an earlier novel, *Rabble in Arms: A Chronicle of Arundel and the Burgoyne Invasion* (1933), Roberts describes the building and deployment of man-of-war gundalows (*Boston, New Haven, Providence, Connecticut, Philadelphia,* and *Spitfire*) to intercept the British invasion down Lake Champlain in 1777. "The point is that gundelos are better than nothing," Benedict Arnold, preparing American defenses, remarks, "Any damned fool can build a gundelo."[18]

In 1960, two novels incorporated the Fort William and Mary raid (and hence gundalows) in their plots. *The Last Gentleman* (1960), by Shirley Barker, a native of New Hampshire, is based on the blasted career of John Wentworth, the last royal governor of the colony. In a colorful scene, she describes "the wallowing, haphazard fleet of gundalows, the water slapping the long sweeps and square bottoms." Soon that gundalow flotilla would capture the fort, an event which greatly undermined Wentworth's power.[19]

Thomas H. Raddall, a Nova Scotian, casts the same materials a little differently in *The Governor's Lady* (1960), a fictional portrait of Frances Wentworth, the governor's promiscuous wife. One of the secondary characters, Michael Wentworth, an ambitious relative of the Wentworth clan from England, blazes away at game birds from his gundalow hidden in the reeds along the Piscataqua. The versatile craft reminded the soldier-sportsman "somewhat of Thames barges." A few chapters later, the Governor "peered with a spyglass toward the gray harbor and the long bulk of Newcastle Island. There seemed to be much activity on the water with boats and gundalows." Like the birds, the Governor learns too late the real purpose of the gundalows. He hears that the fort's defenders have been fooled by the jack-of-all-trades craft which was equally adept at transporting goods, bringing lovers together, serving as a duck blind, or carrying men to capture a fort in a surprise military action.[20]

The gundalow has become a literary convention in American Revolutionary War novels like the Liberty Bell, the Concord Bridge, the *Ranger*, or a Valley Forge hut. Surely such a symbol deserves its own book.

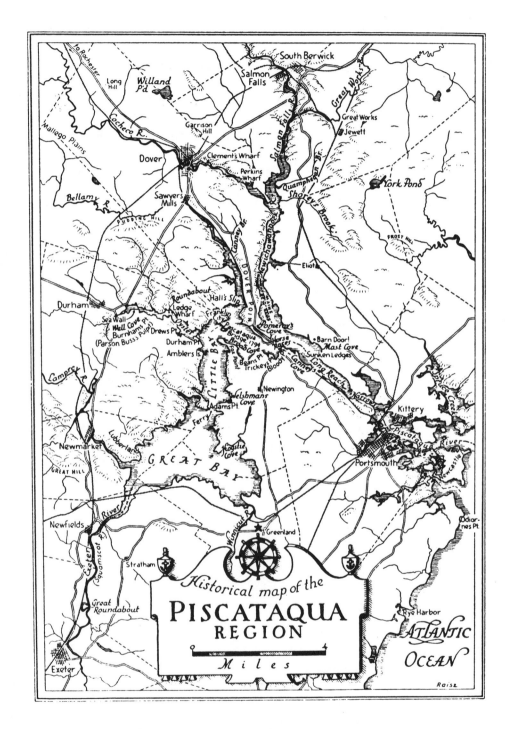

Map of the Piscataqua region, pinpointing gundalow ports and landmarks. HUP.

I Two Hundred and Fifty Years of Gundalowing

The Piscataqua River Basin

THE LAND was ours before we were the land's," observed poet Robert Frost, a longtime New Hampshire resident. A land half-drowned in brackish water determined, more than any other single factor, the history of the Piscataqua River settlers of colonial New Hampshire and Maine. These early pioneers needed to travel through a maze of land and water. For this purpose they developed the gundalow. As a mode of water transportation, the gundalow found a natural home in the Piscataqua River, an estuary of the Atlantic tonguing twenty-five miles inland. Without this local peculiarity of geography, affording such ideal conditions for the nurturing of this vessel, the growth of gundalow transportation would have never developed to the extent that it did.[1]

The "snarling, bubbling, cross-grained" Piscataqua River has its own personality. Spelled as "Piscataqua," "Pascataqua," "Pascataquack," or "Piscataway"—there are approximately twenty variants—the river's name has been translated from the Indian as "a great deer place," "the branch of a river" and "a divided tidal place." In early times the name of Piscataqua "was given not only to the river itself, but also to the entire settlement on both shores, from the mouth upward."[2]

On a map of New Hampshire, one traces the Piscataqua (a salt river in actuality, although streams of fresh water empty into it) from the sea westward into a broad bay. Twice a day a seven-foot tide pushes salt water up into Broad Cove, Little Bay and Great Bay. The Piscataqua River tides "are among the strongest and most powerful in the world." Into these Bays flow five rivers, with waterfalls tumbling over the fall line. Drawing a fine comparison, Charles H. Bell, an Exeter lawyer and one-time governor of the state, observed:

> The river Pascataqua which forms the bound, next the sea, between New Hampshire and Maine, may, with its tributaries, be rudely represented by a man's left hand and wrist laid upon a table, back upwards and fingers wide apart. The thumb would stand for the Salmon Falls or Newichwannock river, the fore-finger for Bellamy river, the second finger for Oyster river, the third for Lamprey river and the fourth for Exeter or Squamscot river; while the palm of the hand would represent the Great Bay, into which most of those streams pour their waters, and the wrist the Pascataqua proper.[3]

The Piscataqua is the confluence of the Cocheco and Salmon Falls Rivers at Dover. The two prongs of this watery divining rod reach for the highland ponds of Strafford County, about forty miles from the sea. The many falls of these two tributaries (Cocheco, the Indian word for "the rapid foaming water") provide ample water power. The whole Piscataqua Basin, in addition to these major rivers, fans out into innumerable coves, bays, peninsulas, islands, marshes, and tidal flats.[4]

In addition to these features, the Piscataqua possesses another attribute to foster a specialized type of watercraft. As David "Bud" McIntosh, a boatbuilder and resident of the Piscataqua area for over seventy years, explains:

> The Northern New England seacoast and the Piscataqua Basin are perhaps the most pleasant places in the world for ships and sailing. There are only three or four rocks along the coast, and every sailor knows where they are. It curves every three or four miles, making for a cove or quick anchorage in case of a storm. And there is a nice mud bottom everywhere.[5]

The existence of a mud bottom almost assures a drunken or confused captain that no harm would befall his vessel in the event of a beaching. Fog is rare and dredging is unnecessary. Furthermore, the Piscataqua basin provides another benefit. Any vessel which continually exposes its hull to salt water risks infestation of worms and barnacles. For any Piscataqua River craft, this problem was easily remedied. As the brackish water gave way to fresh as gundalows continued up into the creeks, the captains not only delivered their goods at the landings before the falls, but also rid their boat bottoms of these borers. "If there were any worms," McIntosh remarks, "a week in fresh water would solve that problem. The worms need salt to live and thrive."[6]

The brackish water itself, the Great Bay, according to a 1708 report, "is furnished with great plenty of fish, such as cod and haddock, ... bass, shad, mackerell, herring, blew-fish, alewifes, pollock, ffrost-fish, perch, fflounders, sturgeons, lumps, ells, hollow-boats, seales, salmon, and many others, and all sorts of shell-fish, such as lobsters, crabs, cockles, clams, mussells, oysters, etc." Gundalowmen ate well, with a catch practically guaranteed with a drop of a line in the early days.[7]

Around the hundreds of miles of shoreline tall white pines, oaks, beeches, and maples once grew skyward. Beneath their limbs beaver, otter, marten, raccoon and fox scampered. The Indians lived here, and paddled around in dugout canoes.

It was not the fish, timber or furs which first brought English exploring parties to the Piscataqua but rather a search for a health cure. In 1603, Martin Pring, sponsored by English merchants, explored along the New England coast in search of sassafras, then considered a cure for syphilis, "the French pox." Entering the Piscataqua, Pring sailed his two ships into the harbor and "rowed up ten or twelve miles." There they stopped and turned around, for "meeting with no sassafras, we left these places."[8]

The other inviting prizes, however, could not be long ignored. Within a decade Samuel Champlain and John Smith explored the region. In 1623 English fishing settlements were established at Odiorne's Point, near the harbor entrance; and at Pomeroy's Cove, close by the tip of Dover Point. Other fishing parties followed and set up their camps. After a slow growth the Piscataqua settlements took firm root, evolving into permanent occupation. In 1653 the citizens of "Strawbery Banke," feeling that the community had outgrown its humble name, desired to call their settlement "Portsmouth" because of its location. By 1659 there is the first authenticated mention of a gundalow, although gundalows undoubtedly existed years before that date. Roughly fifty years after Pring's voyage the Piscataqua River basin was ready for full-scale extraction of its great wealth.[9]

Model of square barge gundalow, built by Clyde Whitehouse, with square sail and sweeps. UNHD.

Adoption of the Gundalow for Transportation Needs

The gundalow proved to be the most logical and best suited craft to serve this business and trading economy. Cheap land transportation was impossible in the jumbled wilderness of land, sea and rivers strewn over primitive maps and charts. The few roads which existed had to circle bays and tidal flats, adding extra miles. Rivers cut off direct access by land, and there were few bridges to span them. As a result, if the area were to survive, "an inexpensive, fast, and direct means of transportation was essential." The gundalow satisfied all three requirements.[10]

Wind and tides offered free power. When oars or "sweeps," as they were called, were used, the gundalow took advantage of the "ash breeze." This propitious wind does not blow in from the Atlantic or down from the White Mountains, but is the human power generated by sweating men, handling the long ashwood oars.[11]

The speed which the gundalows achieved under optimum conditions of fair wind and favorable tide was amazing! They travelled the twenty-five miles from Portsmouth to Exeter in a little over two hours.

The gundalows with their flat bottoms could operate in four feet of water, thus providing direct service to the landings on shallow fresh water creeks. Larger vessels did not dare to attempt such a trip. Those foolish enough to do so, soon found themselves stranded on sand bars. Waiting for the flood tide to arrive, the ships' crews struggled to pull the mired keels loose. Beached gundalows, on the other hand, loosened easily with the tide.

Another asset of the gundalow was its safety. Never intended to be an ocean-going vessel, the gundalow usually remained within the boundaries of the Piscataqua Basin. Land was always in sight. In the event of a storm or fog, it could head for shore and arrive there within minutes. Leaks could be caulked at low tide.

Aside from geography, other local factors brought the gundalow into widespread use. Any farmer with a smattering of carpentry and blacksmithing possessed all the skills required to build one. He used the timber growing on his woodlot. Any wood would do. Built to last about a decade, there was no special concern if the gundalow started to rot. "Ten years of spruce," an old gundalowman once remarked to Bud McIntosh, "and I'm ready for another one." Iron was readily available from the iron works on the Lamprey River. With these local raw materials, the farmer could put his gundalow together over the long winter (for which the Piscataqua area is famous) and have it ready for a spring launching. The initial cost, except for the farmer's time, was next to nothing. Maintenance was cheap and simple; a little patching and caulking here and there were sufficient.[12]

Even the spelling of the name of this craft has the loose anything-will-do-just-as-long-as-it-works casualness associated with its construction. Any spelling or pronunciation will do, and all are correct. There are thirty or forty variations including gondela, gundalow, gundelow, gunlo, gundaloa, and gundeloe. In New England, the word is commonly pronounced in two syllables as "gun 'low." The word, gundalow, is supposedly derived from the Italian, "gondola," used on Venetian canals for passenger travel. Writing in 1883, when the American species was still thriving, John Albee explained:

> You may decline this word: gondola, gondela, gundalow; the first form is pure, the second a variation, the third a corruption. And this order shows also another sort of declension, in the uses to which the craft was put: first, a conveyance for passengers only; second, a similar purpose and sometimes also freight; and last, nothing but rough cargoes of coal and ballast. Words are corrupted as fast as the thing signified comes to an abased use.[13]

This abasement continues into the present day. Although the Piscataqua River gundalow has disappeared, the root word of gondola is still used today in the railroad and construction industries. Nowadays a "gondola" can refer to a railroad car with no top, a flat bottom, and fixed sides for conveying bulk goods or to a motor truck or trailer with hopper-shaped containers for carrying mixed concrete. Like the water carrier, the name (and idea) has not died — it is modified and "abased" to serve modern usage.[14]

Although it is not named as such, the earliest record of a gundalow-like craft in New England appears in a "History of Plymouth Plantation," written by Governor William Bradford during 1630-1646. He noted that "The carpenter/who arrived at Plymouth in 1624/ is an honest and a very industrious man, quickly builds us two very good and strong shallops, with a great and strong lighter. . ." Still defined as a flat-bottomed barge for loading and unloading ships, a lighter was then and is still used in places without adequate docking facilities. During colonial times, barges transported cargoes between the shore and vessels anchored in deeper water. Doubtlessly this lighter was flat-bottomed, with the square ends of a scow. Probably a raft was first used, and then improved enough to warrant the status of a scow. These primitive craft are still in existence today for the unloading of large merchant ships off the Atlantic coast of Africa.[15]

Evolution in Design and Style of the Gundalow

The gundalow evolved from this makeshift beginning. Its development falls into three distinct periods. It is arbitrary to assign definite dates

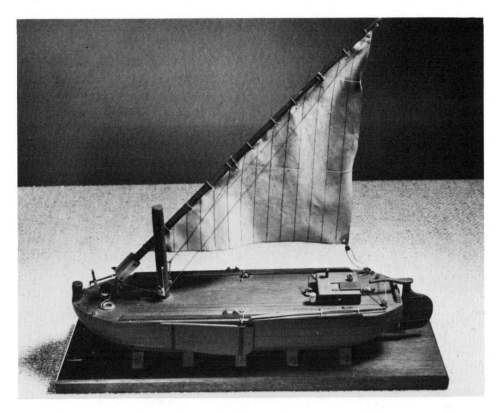

Gundalow model, built by Captain Adams, depicting vessel's mature stage. Note leeboard on port and sweeps carried on deck. Douglas Armsden photo. DAC.

because the first and most primitive type was used throughout the entire gundalow era. Roughly (with loose historical license) these time periods occurred as follows:

1.   (1650-1800). In its infancy, the gundalow was little more than a "dumb" (signifying it had no means of self-propulsion) barge or square-ended scow. It had no attached or permanent rudder, deck or transom. Builders rarely painted it. Before the 1800s it appears that it was rarely rigged for sail. For propulsion, the gundalow captain and his crew used two methods. They either poled along by means of long slim poles or they employed oars, or "sweeps," which were always carried alongside to insure a favorable ash breeze. Comparatively small, the early gundalow was approximately twenty to thirty feet long and had a carrying capacity of ten to twenty cords of wood. When

Model of the Fanny M., *built by Clyde Whitehouse, showing yard and lateen sail. UNHD.*

empty the gundalow drew less than a foot of water; when heavily loaded, about four feet.

2. (1800-1860). During its intermediate stage the gundalow was still a dumb barge, but the builder added a square transom, fixed rudder and usually a tiller. Platforms or decks were at either end. A cuddy, or a small cabin for living quarters, appeared. When sails appeared they were rigged as a single square sail hung from a yard. The mast was removable. Gaining respectability as river craft, the gundalow was now occasionally painted. In 1804 George Spinney printed a notice concerning a "new 10 cord red Gondola." During this middle period gundalows were a common sight on the Piscataqua and its tributaries.

3. (1860-1900). During its last period of development the gundalow achieved its zenith in style and size. The typical gundalow was now sixty feet or more in length and possessed many improve-

ments. Most significantly, a lateen or triangular sail on a yard was adopted from its ancient ancester on the Nile. A stump mast which rotated to take advantage of the wind supported the lateen yard. This arrangement gave the vessel greater steering control as the gundalowman guided his craft in the narrow confines of channels. Another advantage was the ability to drop the lateen sail when passing beneath bridges.

Other features also improved the gundalow's speed and manueverability. Now fully decked, the craft became more streamlined with a spoon bow and a round stern. For steering, the gundalow captain could raise and lower a leeboard on the port side and turn a wheel which was rigged to a permanent rudder by drums and tackle. One old reliable feature was continued—these late gundalows were fitted with long sweeps and poles.

Near the stern the cuddy provided living quarters. Its roof covered a couple of bunks, a stove and an untidy cabin. The larger size required a crew of two or three men.[16]

Despite its ugly duckling appearance the gundalow was a bargain in every sense. As John W. Griffiths, an expert in shipbuilding, wrote in 1875:

> This crude apology for a vessel costs, when complete, about $1500 and we have no hesitation in stating that for river service such as is rendered by these vessels, the same amount of money cannot be invested in another type of vessel which can carry an equal amount of cargo in equal time on the same light draught of water and pass the bridge obstructions which may be encountered without necessitating the opening of draws.[17]

For 250 years the gundalow builders pleased themselves in adapting any shape or form for their craft. In addition to the difficulty of finding an exact description for this protean craft, the number of gundalows which plied Piscataqua estuary can not be precisely determined. All vessels in the Piscataqua region were "enrolled or registered in Portsmouth as the Port of Portsmouth comprised both banks of the Piscataqua." Unfortunately gundalows "were not enrolled and they are not mentioned in custom house records."[18]

The career of the gundalow illustrates an interesting point in maritime history. As D. Foster Taylor explains:

Ship types owe their existence to popular approval. For these reasons the hull and rig of watercraft are rarely stabilized in one form over a long period of time. The primitive type of native boats are known to vary little, but among more enterprising races, constant change and development mark their marine history. Like all watercraft the gundalow existed because of very practical reasons. When conditions changed, and these reasons no longer held, the gundalow faded into the ever growing limbo of ship types along with the frigate, clipper ship and the topsail fishing schooner.[19]

The advent of railroads, motor trucks and power-driven craft doomed the gundalow. With the declining markets of marsh grass, pine masts, cordwood and bricks in the Piscataqua economy the gundalow found itself without a cargo. It could adapt no longer to extend its life. By 1900, hard-headed pragmatism had little patience with the outmoded gundalow and it was abandoned.

The Documentary Gundalow

For the first two centuries of the gundalow's existence, its story resembles the shadowy dimensions of its hull and mast cast by the flickering light of a lantern on the deck during a foggy night. The outline of the gundalow is vaguely recognizable, but with little detail. Scattered documents illuminate but a fraction of the gundalow's remarkable past. Extant papers have outlasted the object they represent. The task of trying to present an accurate account of the gundalow recalls the historical problem of "trying to reconstruct an Egyptian dynasty with only the pharoah's nightshirt for evidence."

Legal documents, particularly wills, memorials and petitions, constitute virtually the only extant records of the early gundalow. Portsmouth newspapers, from 1756 onward, occasionally mention gundalows in their news and advertising columns. Commercial correspondence, especially if carried on by a maritime firm, occasionally contains a bill of transaction about the selling or renting of gundalows. The depository for the bulk of these records, Portsmouth, was swept by three fires, in 1802, again in 1806 and finally by the most devastating one in 1813. Many records were burned. Even gundalow wrecks were virtually ignored. Concerning shipwrecks, "unless they were larger vessels or a loss of life occurred, scant attention appears to be given to them."[20]

In 1659, the first recorded reference states, "Gondolas could come to the foot of the mill/John Cutt's sawmill on Islington Street in Portsmouth/to take away the boards and lumber." Another early reference states that in 1694 William Furber petitioned the Council and received authority "to keep a ferry from his house at Welchman's cove, to transport travellers over to Oyster river, and to receive of passengers, viz. for a man three pence and for horse and man eight pence. . . ." For his ferry service at various landings on the Great Bay, Furber was "to keep attendance and a sufficient boat or gundaloa."[21]

Thanks to the provincial papers concerning the expenditures on Fort William and Mary and referring to the contracted work of Edward Toogood, a Portsmouth gundalow owner and lime and brick supplier, the role of the gundalow can be traced during this period of time. In 1696, during King William's War against France — a conflict which deeply affected the Piscataqua region—Toogood's "Gundeloe" was pressed into service to carry Colonel Gidney's soldiers across the Piscataqua from Portsmouth to the Province of Maine, then a part of Massachusetts. "In so doeing," Toogood's appeal reads, he "hath lost 3 oares . . . an one planke . . . and for emtying of her she being sunke wth water." Justice of the Peace Thomas Parker "Allowed of this Bill 15 Shill."[22]

A year later, in 1697, much work was done on the fort to bolster its defénses. More than thirty men worked on construction. For transporting stone to the fort in their gundalows, Toogood, Thomas Holland, Samuel Hill, Thomas Packer and Elihu Gunnison were paid four shillings a day. During 1703-1705, with the outbreak of Queen Anne's War, the Province of New Hampshire expended more than 453 pounds on the fort. Along with Toogood's "Bricks and Lyme," mason work, "Cutting of Sodds," "Fyne Iron & Nails," the government paid Madam Packer and Samuel Hill for "Gondolo hire." As late as 1722, Toogood continued to be the province's favored contractor for this job. In that year, he charged more than nineteen pounds for two month's work, including his familiar charge, "to 1 Day my self getting of gunelo & telling Bricks."[23]

During peacetime, gundalow ferries continued to be in demand. In 1717, Nicholas Harford "had liberty to keep a ferry from Beck's slip to Kittery, with a sufficient boat or gundalo for the safe transportation of man and horse. . ." Bridges were the special bane of the gundalowmen, who regarded such developments bad for business and safety. In 1726 New Castle Island favored building a bridge across Little Harbor. Portsmouth and Rye in vigorous protest argued:

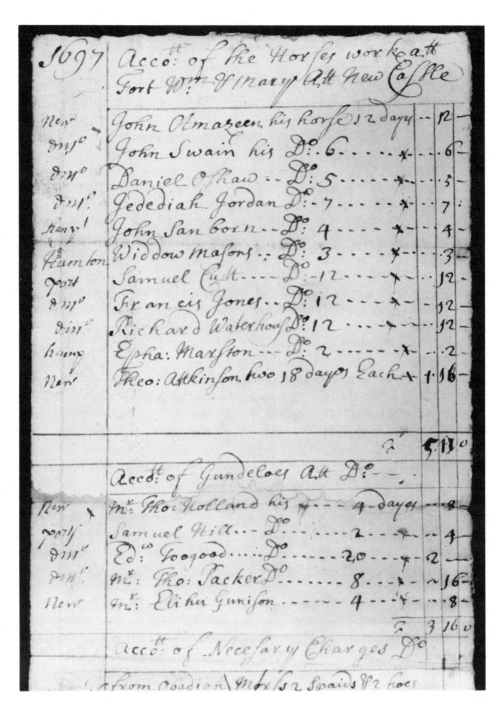

Ledger of the New Hampshire provincial assembly, listing payments to gundalowmen for work at Fort William and Mary during 1697. NHA.

Another unspeakable hardship which will attend a bridge is ye transportation of Hay from ye meadows and marshes where the tides must be attended both by night and day; and to pass under a draw bridge or through any such gap as their may be with a GONDELA of hay in a dark night and a strong wind or in any other vessel with so strong a current as there is besides must needs be a danger too terrible to be thought on.[24]

The gundalow lobby succeeded for the time being; no bridge appeared there until 1759.

During this era the Piscataqua region, as the center of the mast trade for English warships, reverberated with the sounds of axes against tall pines. Gundalows carried out the many activities associated with this industry. Since 1676, the Pepperrell family of Kittery had amassed a fortune in their interrelated empire of land ownership, ship building, fishing, carriers of lumber, livestock, masts, other naval stores and even slaves. After William Pepperrell, the elder, died in 1734 his son, Colonel William, added to the family wealth. During the 1730s and 1740s, the Colonel, continuing the family tradition as Piscataqua's leading merchant, frequently "hiered" gundalows at five to ten shillings a day. Other prominent names in Portsmouth's history at that time, George Jaffrey, Mark Hunking Wentworth and Timothy Gerrish, competed for hiring the available gundalows at the going inflated rate.[25]

The outbreak of King George's War in 1739 brought the Piscataqua economy into a burst of activity. To defend its land against France and Spain in this war, the New Hampshire provincial government "paid out of the Publick Treasury out of the Money Laid in Repair of Fort W^m & Mary" more than sixty pounds to reimburse Andrew Wiggin in 1744. (Toogood had apparently left the scene by this time.) Included in Wiggin's bill were "Expenses to the Workmen & Gundulow." The entire cost of repair was 1688 pounds, with 55 of that figure going "To Sundry Gundelomen." Another document lists "propper men to manage the Gondulo's for Transporting Sods to the Fort William & Mary."[26]

The Piscataqua country could not idly stand by when Colonel William Pepperrell was made commander-in-chief of the expedition to capture Louisburg, the "Dunkirk of America." "Louisburg must be destroyed" became a war cry. Some 500 New Hampshire men accompanied Pepperrell. Their objective was to capture Louisburg, located on the east coast of Cape Breton Island. Since the French had taken

To His Excell.y Benning Wentworth Esq.r

Governour and Commader in Chief, in and over His Maj.ties

Province of New Hampshire in New England, To the Hon.ble His

Majesties Councill for Said Province and House of Repre-

sentatives now Convend in General Assembly —

Charles Hight of Portsmouth in Said Province Sailemaker

humbly Sheweth —

That on the 9th day of December last Past, M.r Samuel

Penhallow Comissary took the complainans Gundulow into the Province

Service for carrying Provisions &c.a to Dover, where Said Gundulow

was keept all Winter, and lost the Anchor & Road & plank belonging

to her, and also Stove in one of her Sides, and other Damage

done her and not returnd to him as yet, and when returnd (unless

repaird will Cost your Complain.t a Considerable Sum of Money to repaire

besides the Loss of her Service this Spring and Summer Season —

Your Complainant humbly Prays your Excellency & Hon.rs

to consider the Premises. and to allow Some compotent Sume

to Satisfie him in reason for the Loss and damage

Sustaind, So Prays your humble Petitioner &c.a —

Portsmouth May

21 - 1747 —

Chas Hight,

[Printed in substance (?) XVIII, p. 309]

In Council May 21 1747

Read and Ord.r to be laid before the Comittee of War for the

Canada Expedition, who are hereby directed to adjust

the affair above.d in the best manner they can

Theodore Atkinson Sec.ry

Laid down for Concurrence

In y.e House of Representatives 18 June 1747 —

Voted that y.e above order of y.e Hon.ble Council be concurrd

D.Peirce &c

Memorial of Charles Hight, Portsmouth, to Governor Benning Wentworth in 1747, seeking redress for damage to his gundalow. Note authorization at bottom of full reimbursement by the New Hampshire House of Representatives. NHA.

twenty-five years in building it, Louisburg was considered impregnable. Yet Pepperrell overcame all obstacles and captured Louisburg in 1745, ending, for all intents and purposes, the war in North America. Peace was signed in 1748.

The role of the Piscataqua gundalow is fully documented in calculating the war costs. As bureaucrats and file clerks of any victorious government know, every war brings home in its wake, along with returning troops, a flood of documents. Petitions and memorials from widows, pension requests from wounded and sick militiamen, and every conceivable claim, legitimate or fraudulent, from injured parties arrive by the basket loads. The battle of paper continues on long after the last shots of any war.

During King George's War, Charles Hight, a Portsmouth sailmaker, fired off two claims to Governor Benning Wentworth of New Hampshire for just compensation. On 24 January 1747 at Portsmouth, the capital of the Province, the House of Representatives:

> Voted that Charles Hight be allow'd three Pounds twelve shillings & Eleven Pence farthing in full for his Acc^t for reparing ye Fort Boat, hire of his Gundloe taking powder out of Capt Hammond &c. to be paid out of ye money in the Treasury. Sent up by Capt. Leavit.[27]

Encouraged with this first settlement, Hight wanted more. Written by an amanuensis in a careful hand and signed by Hight, this manuscript exists in excellent condition. Wentworth in his own hand acknowledged receipt of the petition on the reverse.

> Charles Hight of Portsmouth in said Province Sailemaker humbly shewth—
> That on the 9th day of December last Past, Mr. Samuel Penhallow Comissary took the complainant Gundulow into Province Service for carrying Provissions &C to Dover, where said Gundulow was kept all Winter, and loss of anchor & Boad & plank belonging to her, and also Stove in one of her Sides, and other Damage done her and not returned to him as yet and when returnd (unless repair'd[)] will Cost your Complaint a Considerable Sum of Money to repaire besides the Loss of her Service this Spring and Summer Season...[28]

Theodore Atkinson, Secretary of the Province, scrawled in an overworked and indifferent bureaucratic hand toward the bottom of the page:

> In Council May 21 1747 read and ord^d to be laid before the Committee of War for the Canada Expedition who are hereby Directed to adjust the affair above in the best manner they can[.][29]

At the bottom of the long document, D. Peirce, writing on behalf of the House of Representatives on 18 June 1747:

> Voted that the above order of the Honb^l Council be concurred.

Toward the end of this conflict in 1747, the New Hampshire House considered a more far-reaching petition. For many years the citizens of Newfields, a village between Newmarket and Exeter, sought to build a bridge over the Squamscot River. Fording at low tide or depending upon transient ferriage caused inconvenience and delay. The lines of battle were again drawn among the various towns over the building of this bridge. The communities of Newfields and Nottingham pitted themselves against Exeter, Stratham, Kensington, Hampton Falls, Epping, East Kingston, and Brentwood. Among other objections, an Exeter petition on May 13 stated that the proposed bridge "would also make it very Dangerous to pass with Vessells rafts & Gundelows in the Narrow Passage Thirty foot." On 4 June 1747, the General Assembly approved a Committee's proposal to build the bridge, but, nevertheless, recommended "a Passage for Vessels Gundelos Rafts and other water Carriage be Left where the Deepest Water is of forty feet wide Between the Peers."[30]

Despite winning the battle, the citizens of Newfields lost the bridge war, since its backers apparently did not have the funds to build it. The bridge was not built until about 1775. But this presage of new times must have warned the gundalow captains that they must soon make technological changes in their gundalows if they were to survive.

These new times were symbolized in part by the establishment of the first newspaper in New Hampshire. On 7 October 1756 in Portsmouth, Daniel Fowle printed the first issue of the *New-Hampshire Gazette*. From then on information about gundalows in the oldest continuously printed newspaper in the United States becomes more plentiful. On 13 October 1758 two gundalows were advertised for sale in that city, "one of which is extream good, and will carry sixteen Cord Wood."

A few years later a reward of one dollar was offered for the return of a small gundalow which went "adrift from Mr. Sherburne's wharf."[31]

Throughout the colonial era, the gundalow played a vital part in Piscataqua's commerical and military development.

The Gundalow in the American Revolutionary War

Early gundalowmen were well acquainted with New Castle (formerly Great) Island and the fortification there. Located at the river's mouth, its strategic position commands Portsmouth harbor.

By 1632 the English had built a rudimentary fort on the northeast point. Since that time this site has been used as a military base. Today the United States Coast Guard administers this rocky promontory. Known as "the Castle" for a long time, these defensive works were renamed in 1694 as Castle William and Mary, after the popular reigning British monarchs who had donated new artillery. It was never a Louisburg in military strength; the British government was generally stingy in appropriations, leaving the neglected fort in disrepair. Although "in disreputable condition," Fort William and Mary, as it became known by 1774, was still the strategic key to New Hampshire.[32]

Throughout 1774 uneasiness gripped the citizens of Portsmouth, as an approaching storm. Sympathy for the citizens of Boston, the refusal to allow an English ship to unload its chests of tea in Portsmouth, and the dispersal of a local Committee of Correspondence to Exeter (where it re-assembled in secret) created tension. Governor John Wentworth, Benning Wentworth's successor, was losing control.

On Tuesday, 13 December 1774 at about four in the afternoon, Paul Revere rode into Portsmouth with a message from the Boston Committee of Correspondence. When Revere found his local contact, Samuel Cutts of the Portsmouth Committee, the two men "went into Stoodleys Tavern together." What or how much they drank is not known, but their topic of conversation was heady stuff. This meeting sealed the fate of Fort William and Mary.[33]

Cutts learned that the British government had ordered all colonial governors to prevent munitions from entering the American colonies. Patriots in Rhode Island, Revere reported, had responded to this edict by seizing the armaments at Fort George in Newport harbor. The purpose of Revere's ride, a practice run for his more famous ride to Lexington four months later, was to warn the Portsmouth Committee that British troops might be sent to prevent a similar action in Portsmouth. Alarmed by this rumor, Cutts soon spread the word.

The next day, December 14, "a Drum and fife pervaded the streets of Portsmouth, accompanied by several Committee-men, and the Sons of Liberty." A short distance away at his comfortable residence, almost within earshot of the commotion, Governor Wentworth heard a noise at the door. "At noon my servant came in," Wentworth wrote, "and told me Drums were beating for men to attack the Castle and that fifty were already embark'd in a Gondula."[34]

At Fort William and Mary, Captain John Cochran manned the post with six soldiers. "It was very cold" that day, and later the gray sky turned to snow. The Captain, as he sat by the fire, was not overly suspicious of anything out of the ordinary. When various "Mariners" approached the fort, Cochran's wife, Sarah, brought him his "Pistols well charged." Soon "John Langdon of Portsmouth, Merchant," in the words of Cochran's deposition, "said if I would let him and one other Gentleman in, they would let Me know their Business..." Langdon, the leader of four hundred men, many picked up on the way from Kittery and New Castle, had landed at the Castle. They employed gundalows to make the trip from the center of Portsmouth.[35]

An analysis of Langdon's plan of attack on the fort reveals that this military operation was no ragtag affair of half-drunken men streaming out of Stoodley's Sign of the King's Arms and the Bell Tavern. As a one-time ship captain, Langdon was well versed in gundalows and their capabilities. The beating of the drum at noontime was a pre-arranged signal for the volunteers to meet at these taverns, prior to heading for the riverfront for embarkation in the gundalows for an amphibious operation against the fort. Patriots from across the river in Kittery coordinated their timing to arrive in their gundalows simultaneously at the fort. The gundalows up river simply took advantage of the ebb tide for their trip to the fort. Patriots who lived on New Castle Island or who were already there by that early afternoon simply joined Langdon's landing party. At that time a single bridge connected the Island to the mainland. Tramping from Rye to the south of Portsmouth, these men used the bridge across Little Harbor and continued on the road to the fort. Aiding Langdon's plans was a lucky circumstance; the weather reduced the visibility for the fort's defenders. The element of surprise in this entire maneuver served Langdon well.[36]

England's long neglect in maintaining the fort with adequate troop strength and proper equipment cost her dearly. Its defense was pitiful. Captain John Cochran was a mariner, not a soldier, and com-

In a diorama at the State Capitol, John Langdon in black cape defying the British in his 1774 raid on Fort William and Mary. Note gundalows on left. Bill Finney photo. NHSH.

manded a token force of six men. Cochran's men were, moreover, conscripts rather than regulars.

Langdon's band of four hundred men, to be sure, was not a professional army. To the contrary, this group of men has long been characterized by historians as little more than a mob, a street gang, the riffraff of the town. Depositions by Cochran and his men reveal, however, that Langdon's raiding party consisted of many officers in the New Hampshire militia as well as leading merchants and ship captains of Portsmouth. These men were skilled in the use of muskets and gundalows.[37]

It was now about three in the afternoon. The skies began to spit snow. Langdon demanded the powder; Cochran refused. The issue was quickly decided. In Cochran's words, "Great Numbers assembled on Every Side the Fort and in an Instant the signal was given for storming where upon I ordered the Men to fire. They instantly discharged the Cannon and small Arms, but the Soldiers being in too much haste they had no Effect. . . . two hundred Men . . . scaled the Walls instantly and others still coming forward, it became impossible to withstand such a Multitude." The storming parties carried the works and captured Cochran and his tiny force. Denied the keys, Langdon's men broke open the "Door of the Powderhouse with an Iron Crow Bar." They then carried away "about one hundred Barrels of Powder...leaving only one Barrel behind." The timing worked out perfectly. Since the sun did not set until 4:28 P.M. the patriot band had enough daylight to lug the barrels down to the shore. There they "embark'd it [the powder] in Gondulas, and carried it off upon the flood Tide in about one hour and half."[38]

A contemporary letter, published in the *New-Hampshire Gazette* on December 23, carries the story a little further. After the men "took possession of 97 [actually 98] barrels of Powder," they "put it on board the Gundalow, bro't it up to Town, and went off with it to some Distance in the Country." Leaving this cargo in Portsmouth, subject to the possibility of recapture, would have been a blunder. Using gundalows to carry the five tons of powder to the inland bay villages insured its safety, beyond the reach of the British forces. Anchored at Boston at the time, the two armed British ships, *Canceaux* and *Scarborough*, could not have given proper chase even had they been on the Piscataqua that day. Their bulky hulls would have struck bottom while the flat-bottomed gundalows navigated the fresh water creeks.[39]

News of this first raid on Fort William and Mary spread as fast as the flood tide extended into the Bays. John Sullivan, a well-to-do Durham lawyer and mill owner, had recently returned to his home as a representative from New Hampshire in the Continental Congress. His hillside home overlooked Oyster River Landing, an inland port alive with gundalows and other craft. Sullivan's brother James, in fact, had been "engaged in gondolaing" on the Piscataqua in his youth. Sullivan quickly became the leader of the patriot forces of the inland villages, and certainly knew the capabilities of gundalows for any military plans he might have had. In a 1785 newspaper statement, Sullivan claimed that the powder in the gundalows was eventually sent "to my care; which myself and others deposited in places of security." Hearing "that two vessels of war were coming from Boston to take possession of the fort and harbour," Sullivan decided to act. Taking the powder was only half the battle, he believed. The remaining military supplies at the fort, Sullivan felt, must be seized as well.[40]

It appears that Sullivan spent most of the morning of December 15 in preparation for his expedition. According to the memory of Captain Eleazer Bennett, (the last survivor of this party who gave his account of this event at the age of 101), Sullivan and his men approached Benjamin Mathes, the owner of a "gondola" at Durham. Too old to accompany this expedition, or perhaps too sensible to consider it, Mathes stayed behind and let Sullivan's force board her for the trip "down the river from Durham to Portsmouth."[41]

At Portsmouth during that same morning, Governor Wentworth was fast becoming an emperor without clothes. Meeting with his Council, Wentworth attempted to "enlist or impress thirty men for defence of the Castle." His efforts to raise a loyalist force were fruitless. When Sullivan and over 500 men arrived in Portsmouth that afternoon, Wentworth's power was fast eroding.[42]

Negotiations between Wentworth and Sullivan broke down. Rumors, reports, speeches, and drinking continued. About seventy men accompanied Sullivan to Jacob Tilton's Bell Tavern and waited for the ebb tide. A messenger brought the news that a thousand men were marching into town, including 600 from Berwick and Kittery. With this news, "Major Sullivan proceeded to embark His party in gondulas & the tide being suitable, landed at Newcastle at 10 o'clock." There they joined the Kittery and Berwick contingents. "A cold, clear moonlight night" aided the attackers. There was no turning back now. Sullivan's commitment to this action was financial as well; he later admitted, "I bore the expense of all the party."[43]

Upon his arrival, Sullivan told Captain John Cochran that his forces "were all Men of property and were coming with intent to Carry off the Province stores." This time Cochran and his six soldiers offered no resistance. Through the night, Sullivan's forces "Continued at work taking away the Cannon and stores without any Distinction, and bore them down to the gondalows." The booty consisted of "Sixteen pieces of Cannon, ten Carriages and about forty two Musquets with shot," as well as "bayonets, and cartouch-boxes ... and ordnance stores." Until nine o'clock the next morning, December 16, Sullivan and his men stripped the fort of everything of military value except the heaviest guns.[44]

"The tide now making up" was the moment on that morning Sullivan's gundalow flotilla awaited. They waded out into the water, pushed off, and "came to the upper part of the Town (Portsmouth), when the tide failed them." There Colonel Nathaniel Folsom, commanding "a large Squadron of arm'd Infantry and Cavalry," was waiting to guard these military stores. Apparently they never unloaded the gundalows, but waited until the river's tide turned. At nine o'clock in the evening when "the Tide served upward," Sullivan pushed off again.[45]

His gundalows reached the mouth of the Durham, or Oyster, River which was "frozen over." That did not stop him. "After several

"Landing at the Falls" (1935), representing Durham Town Landing on the Oyster River from the grounds of General John Sullivan's house. Ink and watercolor by Stuart Travis. GB.

days spent in cutting the ice," Sullivan guided his gundalows through the freed channel and docked at the landing. The stores were quickly unloaded. According to tradition, the bulk of the powder was originally lodged under the pulpit of the Durham meeting-house and a portion was taken by Major John Demerit to his house. In a short time, however, the raiders re-distributed the powder and stores throughout southeastern New Hampshire.[46]

Back in Portsmouth, Wentworth received military reinforcements when the two English ships arrived from Boston to neutralize the "Castle," now a mere symbol, worthless to either side without its armaments. The armed ship *Canceaux* arrived on Saturday evening, December 17, and the man of war *Scarborough*, two days later. But the powder was gone. *Scarborough*, in a show of force, laid waste to the fort. Langdon's and Sullivan's raids on Fort William and Mary marked the effective end of the rule of Governor John Wentworth. Although he remained in power until the following summer, Wentworth was, in one writer's words, "helpless, caught like a piece of driftwood in the Piscataqua current."[47]

The gundalow proved to be the perfect military craft for these raids. Fast, maneuverable, and able to take advantage of the tides and the shallow rivers upstream, the gundalow served both as a landing craft for troops and as a cargo vessel.

In June 1775, again according to tradition, Major John Demerit of Madbury hitched up an oxen team at his home and "Took a cart load of powder" some sixty miles south to Bunker Hill. He arrived just in time to supply powder to the colonial forces. Whether or not the tradition is true, it is probable that some of the Fort William and Mary powder, secreted away and stored as late as April in Kingston, Epping, Nottingham, Brentwood, Londonderry, Portsmouth, and Exeter, found its way southward for this battle.

Despite its vast damage, the Americans repaired Fort William and Mary. A company of musketeers, supported by artillery, manned its walls. But since the site was vulnerable to the guns of British warships, the Americans devised a more flexible and sophiscated strategy to defend Portsmouth. Once again, the humble gundalow played an important role.

In the fall of 1775, Brigadier General John Sullivan, his higher rank undoubtedly due to his successful raid, took leave of General George Washington at Continental Army headquarters in Cambridge, Massachusetts. At Washington's command, Sullivan returned to his native area to speed the defenses of Portsmouth. To execute Washington's orders, Sullivan looked over the natural topography of the harbor. At the "Narrows" of the Piscataqua River, below the town, Peirce's and Seavey's Islands pinch the river to create a tremendous current. Even during peacetime in colonial days, Henderson's Point, projecting from Seavey's Island, made navigation difficult. The gundalowmen and ship captains referred to this rock ledge, which caused the dangerous current, as "Pull-and- be-Damned Point." On Seavey's Island, Fort Sullivan, named for the general, was nearing completion. Across the Narrows on Peirce's Island, another set of earthworks, Fort Washington, was being built.

Sullivan analyzed this situation and tackled a number of projects at once. Under his direction, the harbor fortifications soon bristled with a defense in-depth-plan. With the guns of both forts facing the river, any enemy ship approaching the harbor would be under an enfilading fire pattern. The guns covered a massive log boom. Between the forts and the boom, Sullivan positioned fireships—small boats stuffed with combustibles. He had to provide direct access to Peirce's Island from the Portsmouth side of the river. In his lengthy report to Washington, dated 29 October 1775 Sullivan explained, "I immediately Collected a Number of Gondalows moored them head & stern Laid pieces from one to the other & Plank across & Soon Compleated the Bridge." This pontoon bridge, connecting the island to the mainland, constituted the first link between the two points of land. Now workmen, musketeers, and cannoneers walked to their posts. The British never breached Sullivan's elaborate defenses during the war, thanks in part to the pontoon bridge, certainly one of the earliest in American military history.[48]

The role of the gundalow in the Revolutionary War, perhaps related to this very bridge, is documented by a claim submitted to the New Hampshire Committee of Safety. Sitting in session in Exeter, this group replaced the Wentworth regime as the governing body for the former colony. On 16 July 1776 the Delegates "Order'd The Receiver General To pay Mr Wm Coffin Nine pounds 6/7 L. My, for the hire of his Gundelo & the pay for Lumber for fire rafts, as Pr his Acct."[49]

In many New England homes, the tradition of hanging the family ancestor's Revolutionary War musket over the fireplace continues to this day. While a family gundalow would not be as handy and practical, even if it were preserved, the gundalow likewise contributed toward winning the Revolutionary War.

Building and Navigation

During war and peace the Piscataqua farmers kept building gundalows, an activity as traditional as spring planting and mending stone walls. Every gundalow was unique, built without a fixed set of plans, safety requirements or specified materials. Builders measured in their heads, not on paper. To press for exactness in any account about gundalows smacks of assigning precision to an imprecise form. Like snowflakes, everyone was different.

The most complete account of the construction of any gundalow describes the *Fanny M.*, built by Edward H. Adams at Adams Point during the 1880s. During this age of energy conservation and do-it-yourself construction in a backyard or garage, anyone who would like to learn more about or to build his own gundalow and who is concerned with the technical names and dimensions of every piece of lumber and metal fixture, down to the last iron staple, should consult D. Foster Taylor's detailed article, "The Gundalow *Fanny M.*" That article is written for a specific audience.[50] The following account attempts to cover the fundamental points for the layman.

During the 1600s and 1700s farmers were practically the sole builders of gundalows, but during the 1800s, as this craft became more specialized and complicated, professional shipwrights constructed them in boatyards at South Berwick, Maine. Since the workers in these yards concentrated on gundalows as a business, these commerically built boats varied less.[51]

Selecting and cutting the timbers was the first step in gundalow construction. For days the farmer would search the woods to locate trees with a crooked or bent shape for the knees and bow logs. Likely places to look were riverbanks with trees extending over the water.

For the heavy members of the frame, such as the knees and floor timbers, oak was the best wood. Larch trees, or "hackmatack," a balsam poplar, were also satisfactory. The planking and corner pieces were usually spruce. For working the crooked stuff, the builder relied on his adze and broad-axe. The straight logs, required for the clamps, floors, and deck timbers, were taken by boat downriver to a saw mill and cut to size. All the trunnels, or wooden nails, were made by hand. The builder spent many hours making hundreds of trunnels and drilling 1½ inch holes for them.[52]

Blacksmithing contributed the iron work. For the banding around the rudder, sweep locks, bar for the leeboard and so forth, the

Robert Eger using an adz to shape a gundalow knee, carved from a hackmatack buttress root. Bob LaPree photo. NHT.

Bottom planking and floor with cross timbers, connected by square-end trunnels, during the initial stage of construction of the Captain Edward H. Adams. *The trunnel ends will then be cut flush. UNHD.*

average farmer possessed a limited knowledge of smithing or took this job to someone nearby. The basic processes of the trade consist of tapering, upsetting (or making it bigger), and welding, — techniques which have been known for hundreds of years and are easy to learn. The old-timers used charcoal for fires at their forges. For making holes in wrought iron they used a punch. If a part cracked while it was hot, the old-timer probably had to re-cast the whole piece. "If they didn't have one piece," one modern blacksmith remarks, "they would make do with two pieces." But exact or inexact, makeshift or precise, the gundalow builder forged the necessary hardware for his craft.[53]

For a shallow draft, the gundalow had no keel. This flat bottom gave the boat the ability, if need be, to "sail over a heavy dew." The most difficult part of making the frame was shaping the spoon-like bow and forming the corner sections. Ten or twelve logs were required. Because logs fell short, braces of proper natural curvature were fitted in position. The corner pieces, or chine logs, united the floor and sides and gave shape to the craft. The gundalow hull was built up, floor planking laid on, and all the various knees, planks and floors were fastened together with trunnels.

Bow of the Fanny M. *Whitehouse model, showing the cutwater and stump mast. UNHD.*

"It's cheaper to pump than caulk," maintains an old river adage. The gundalowman, however, employed a technique even cheaper than pumping. When it was necessary to drain water from the vessel the gundalow captain simply headed for the nearest sand bar or mud bottom. Within a half day, of course, the outgoing tide would leave her high and dry. The crew would pull the plugs in drain holes drilled through the corner pieces. Nature drained the vessel, and the plugs were redriven. Forgetting to reinsert the plugs before the arrival of the incoming tide, on the other hand, represented the devilish side of nature's free pump. On 8 September 1798 Joseph Young of Dover "went on board a loaded gondola at the Landing, in order to watch her till high water." Since he was tired, he went down into the cuddy and fell asleep "till the tide came up and filled her, by which he was drowned."[54]

For the original caulking, old rags dipped in the grease of rancid salt pork served well. Re-caulking a leaky gundalow was awkward, owing to the flat bottom of the vessel, which was rarely exposed. Once the bottom was tipped to the correct angle, the crew quickly and easily "would get some sawdust and mud, and shove it up into the cracks and holes." The planking on the vessels was at least four inches thick. Pine, spruce and oak were the best woods for this part of the gundalow. "Pine would swell," one authority asserts, "and they wouldn't have to caulk it as much as some of the others."[55]

The rail around the deck was made of oak. For the deck of the gundalow, however, "the flats" were always laid with white pine. Members of the crew stood on the deck, performing their duties or working the long forty foot sweeps, and needed maximum traction. Oak is slippery when wet, and pine assured the best footing. Sideboards, which could be removed, held in the cargo. A slight crown on deck amidships provided sufficient slope for shedding rain.

A rudder and tiller enabled the captain to steer the gundalow. The leeboard, traditionally secured to the hull on the port side, could "be adjusted up and down to prevent being caught on the bottom."[56]

The rigging of the gundalow was, perhaps, its most striking and noticeable feature. The lateen, or leg-of-mutton, sail was supported by a spruce yard about 65 to 70 feet long, tapered toward the end. The yard, or spar, was usually the length of the gundalow. A short rotating stump or short oak mast, usually 15 to 20 feet high, supported the yard. An iron bushing on the end of the mast helped to prevent the wood from splitting.

The sail was a triangular piece of cotton duck with an area of about one thousand square feet. Secured to the yard, the sail had two rows of reef points and five brail lines. Brailing or rolling up the sail was necessary in squalls and when tipping the yard completely down to pass under bridges.[57]

Anchors and ground tackle completed the basic equipment. These items, made out of cast iron of the patent variety, were of considerable weight. The anchor weighed approximately 200 pounds, and the 140 feet of chain, about 500 pounds.

Painting, if practical or desired, completed the job. Since paint was scarce, many gundalows never saw paint during their days on the river. A farmer typically used the most readily available color, usually matching his barn. Red barns accounted for red gundalows. The bottoms were rarely painted, since frequent groundings on mud banks quickly scraped off every vestige of paint. But the aesthetic appeal of the gundalow was comparatively unimportant. It was built for utility and a life of hard work on the river.

After a winter of construction the farmer and his work crew launched the gundalow in the spring. Teams of oxen dragged the gundalow to a mud bank where the incoming tide picked it up. Gundalows were generally worked in the rivers and bays from March or April to November or December. Some adventurous captains continued longer, and occasionally their gundalows were caught and frozen in ice for the winter as a result of their daring. Contemporary records of the Frost family in Durham, dating from 1806 to 1833, contain many references to "when the river closes up," or "as long as the river is open."[58]

Once underway, the gundalows shuttled up and down the river at remarkable speed. "Down on one tide and home on the next," ran a river saying. They not only could make good time with the wind, but would also work to windward with the assistance of their large leeboards.[59]

"Shooting the bridges" remains the most commonly remembered technique of gundalow navigation. This feat inspired much bragging from the river men. The "Piscataqua Rig," a Yankee invention unique in the sailing world, expedited this feat. Sailing right up to a bridge, the captain would give the order to lower the yard and sail at the last possible second. The yard was "loosely chained to the short mast so that the sail could be quickly lowered as the craft coasted under the bridge." The forward momentum propelled the gundalow for a few seconds without loss of speed. Once the bridge was cleared, a "counterweight at the lower end" of the yard quickly raised the sail. With this accomplished, the gundalow continued on its way. Aside from impressing admiring spectators, "shooting the bridge" saved time and displayed Yankee engineering on the river at its best.[60]

Such ingenuity allowed fast runs. The established record from Newmarket Landing to Portsmouth "and return was six and one quarter hours." When the wind failed, the crew resorted to the sweeps and poles. To assure safe passage across shallow areas, the gundalowmen at the beginning of spring "set out stakes at low tide marking channels." On the top of each marker, they fixed a piece of white cloth to assist nighttime navigation.[61]

Whenever a problem arose in the construction and navigation of a gundalow, its solution was quickly forthcoming. Relating such an incident, Captain Edward H. Adams of the *Fanny M.* recalled a potentially dangerous situation. As the *Fanny M.* once approached a bridge in a stiff breeze and unsettled conditions, Adams realized his most prudent act would be to pull over to a little landing place, just before the bridge pilings, tie up at this haven and wait out the storm. Otherwise his gundalow had a good chance of smashing against the pilings.

"Frenchy," he yelled to his hired man. "Heave a bowline."

"I've got to learn real quickly how to tie a bow."

In his fluster and agitation, Frenchy frantically tied some kind of a loop knot. Whether it was a true bowline doesn't matter. His makeshift knot served its purpose and the vessel docked safely. Such resoluteness exemplifies the spirit of improvised navigation on the river.[62]

Routes of Trade

The gundalow, once built and riverworthy, was engaged in a highly competitive struggle for trade routes. Affecting the commerce of southeastern New Hampshire, and in turn, the watercraft transporting it, were the decisions being made in the commercial circles of Boston. After the Revolutionary War Massachusetts businessmen saw that New York was the market for goods from southern New England and "that their most likely competitor for trade to the north was Portsmouth." Going one step further, these Boston merchants decided to increase their volume of business by tapping the trade of southern New Hampshire. To this end, they dug the Middlesex Canal to provide direct access to the Merrimack River Valley region. The canal extended seventy-five miles north of Boston to Concord, New Hampshire. Thus the Concord, Manchester, and Nashua manufacturers and merchants realized that the natural outlet for their goods was no longer the old west-east connection over roads to the Piscataqua region. The Merrimack River, the canal and eventually the railroad created a permanent north-south trade route in the Merrimack Valley, capturing the Piscataqua business. This development caused the Piscataqua gundalowmen to be even more competitive to retain what trade was left to them. Boston not only siphoned off the trade, but also appropriated the idea for the carrier to transport these goods. The Middlesex Canal interests copied the basic form and style of the gundalow for their own sailing barges engaged in river freighting. Except for its smaller dimensions, dictated by the

An 1867 invoice of W. H. and G. K. Drew, Dover, New Hampshire, for packet and gundalow freighting service. UNHMS photo. RWC.

necessity of navigating the canal locks, the canal barge was almost identical to the gundalow. In 1851, the last boat on the Middlesex Canal made its final trip. The railroad had rendered water transport obsolete.[63]

Throughout the years, Piscataqua citizens strove to maintain their tight hold on the bulk of commerce in the bay area. Mast roads, toll roads and bridges appeared, sometimes aiding the gundalow industry, sometimes diverting it. During the years from 1790 to 1820 an era of road and bridge-building fever swept New Hampshire. More than thirty turnpikes were constructed in the state, and fifty bridge companies were incorporated.[64]

The Piscataqua Bridge was begun and completed during 1794, connecting Newington and Durham over Little Bay. Stretching from Fox Point, Newington, across Rock Island and Goat Island to the Durham shore at Meader's Point, the bridge opened trade between Portsmouth and the central part of the state, retaining some of the Salem and Boston trade for the Piscataqua ports. The span was almost a half mile long. This bridge was considered a marvel of engineering in its time. When ice carried off 600 feet of the bridge in February 1855 the owners decided it was too expensive to rebuild it. During its sixty years of service, however, the bridge opened a new highway to Portsmouth and greatly contributed to the prosperity of the town. The first New Hampshire turnpike road became linked to the bridge and helped to create this expansion of business.[65]

Gundalows heading downstream passed under the bridge and approached Bloody Point, as the current began to pick up. The rapids at this site are known as the "Horse Races," where the Piscataqua swings around Bloody Point. Before a railroad bridge was built, this general area was the landing place of many ferries to Dover as well as to Eliot on the Maine side of the river. An important passenger on these early ferries was John Adams, then a young lawyer, on a trip to northern New England in 1770.[66]

Continuing downstream, "Boiling Rock" was very conspicuous at low tide, and represented a particular nemesis to gundalowmen. "They figured," one old-timer recalled:

> when they got past Boiling Rock and to the Portsmouth bridge that they were half way to Boston, no matter where they were going. That rock was a hazard, and they'd watch for it day or night to miss it. And when they passed it, if they had anything to drink everybody would have a drink aboard the ship that they'd safely passed the Boiling Rock.[67]

This rock was in the middle of "Cutts Eddy," considered "the worst in the river for boatmen, especially gundalows." Mentioned as early as 1656 in land documents, Boiling Rock is now gone, not from erosion, but blasted and moved out when the oil tank farms were built on that side of the river.[68]

Soon the "Pulpit" came into view, so called from a rock that hangs out from shore. Boatmen held to a superstition that everyone should offer his respects to the rock, otherwise bad luck would plague the voyage. Some anxious moments gripped them once when John Sullivan was a passenger bound from Durham to Portsmouth. Sullivan, who had already defied the British at Fort William and Mary, continued in character and refused to pay respects to "the devil's pulpit," as he called it, when the rock came into view. Sullivan had done well after the war; he was now Governor of New Hampshire, and apparently unwilling as well to lower the dignity of his office in such a gesture.

"Sir, the birds," said one boatman, "seem to have flown over your hat."

Wearing a tri-colored hat with a plume, Sullivan raised his hand and quickly brought down his hat for inspection.

"I see nothing."

"We've passed the Pulpit, sir."

The stratagem worked, the boatmen resumed their good cheer, and good fortune rested on the voyage for the rest of the day. Otherwise the rock would have undoubtedly broken loose from the cliff and crashed down upon the boat.[69]

In his "A Sail on the Piscataqua," James Kennard, Jr. (1815–1847), a local poet, captured the legend in verse, writing:

Now we're past the Pulpit pressing:
Lift your hat, and bend your head,
To the Parson for his blessing.

Stationed in the rocky bank
From his Pulpit, as we near him.
Through the pine-trees, whispers he
Solemn words, would we but hear him.[70]

On the trip upstream and once past the Pulpit, the gundalowmen quickly lost any superficial piety they might have had. Going up the Long Reach, the beautiful stretch between Boiling Rock and Dover Point, they shouted out, "Barn door," as soon as they caught sight of a barn on a distant hill on the Eliot side, "the doors of which were never known to be shut." The cry was a signal for a dram of rum, and the men "would flat their oars and take their grog, the better to stem the strong current of the Long Reach." At the "Horse Races" they repeated this practice to gain their strength for the swift and powerful current. Finally those continuing up the Oyster River encountered Half-Tide Rock, upon entering the mouth of the stream. To brace for the ordeal of navigating past this rock, they relied upon a third dram. All were happy upon arriving at the Durham Landing.[71]

By relying upon natural and man-made features, the gundalow pilots became skillful in mastering the routes of trade around the Piscataqua region. Yet the biggest landmark, planned to be developed in the middle of this watery empire, has never risen from the visionary plans of its long-dead promotors.

After the completion of the Piscataqua Bridge in 1794 some men petitioned the New Hampshire legislature in 1796 to incorporate Franklin City, a projected settlement at Meader's Neck at the end of Piscataqua Bridge. Comprising approximately 200 acres north of Meader's Neck and nearby Cedar Point, Franklin City would grow as a shipping and trading metropolis in the middle of the Piscataqua region, or so its developers thought when drafting an elaborate map. They envisioned a city with many lots for sale, complete with a court house, meeting house, a combined hall and library and even a State House. The streets were named for heroes of the American Revolution. Had such a city ever materialized, the gundalow would have been its flagship, and in constant demand in this New Hampshire version of Constantinople or Singapore.

Although vessels were built and launched here, the embargo and the War of 1812 checked business, and the subsequent "decline of shipping was a serious blow to the settlement of the proposed city, and the idea was gradually abandoned." The wharves, streets, and house-lots on the map never sprang into reality. One thinks of Martin Chuzzlewit in Charles Dickens' novel of that title (1844) adoring the plans of Eden City in Zephaniah Scadder's office. When Chuzzlewit stepped outside, he saw nothing but a swampy field in Illinois. Similarly Charles Dudley Warner and Mark Twain's *The Gilded Age* (1873) examines the greed of land speculators. Colonel Beriah Sellers in that novel had magnificent plans for his city of Napoleon, but they remained on paper. Franklin City, destined to become the gundalow's greatest landmark and port, never achieved the status of a village. Today residential houses occupy this tract of land. The ghost town of Franklin City is now part of Madbury and Durham.[72]

Cargoes

The variety of cargoes carried in the hulls and on the decks of the gundalows demonstrates the evolution of an increasingly sophisticated economy in the Piscataqua Basin. In the earliest period, cargoes were agricultural and fishing products. Salt hay, fish, lumber, salt and farm produce represented typical goods. A passenger paying his fare was welcome throughout the gundalow era. With the advent of the Industrial Revolution, bricks, stone and lime for the building of the factories, as well as cordwood and coal to fuel them, were profitable cargoes. To operate the

Seabrook farmers unloading a cargo of marsh hay from a gundalow. SHS.

Square-ended gundalow loaded with salt hay on the Parker River, Newbury, Massachusetts. Note sweeps to propel boat. SPNEA.

brickyards, managers needed cordwood for their kilns. The Portsmouth Naval Shipyard, located on Seavey's Island in the Piscataqua harbor, required a constant supply of lumber and naval stores for its ship-building operations. For running the industrial plants at Exeter, Newmarket, Dover, and South Berwick, the gundalow captain transported coal, cotton and textile machinery from Portsmouth, and he returned with finished cloth and forest products. It is ironic that the Piscataqua region, a rich self-sufficient farming and fishing community in its early days, became so revolutionized by and dependent upon manufacturing during the nineteenth century that it could no longer feed itself, and "imported large quantities of flour, corn, butter, and cheese." The gundalow carried these products as well.[73]

Salt hay, certainly one of the gundalow's earliest cargoes, was part of a New England agriculture which has all but vanished since the 1890s. Cattle and horses loved this special fodder, which comprised a major part of their diet. Each fall farmers brought their gundalows to the tidewater marshes to harvest the wild salt grass at neap tide. The horses on board were led off the gundalows. Wearing special shoes, or "bog boots," to prevent being mired, the horses raked up the cut hay into large haystacks resembling beehives. Then the gundalow transported the free crop back home with the incoming tide.[74]

Building stone appears early in business record books as one of the important cargoes. On his farm property, Captain Bradbury Jewell, a citizen of Durham Point, was hampered by a large number of field boulders. But he turned this obstacle to his crops into a profit. This granite, or "gneiss" as it is called, proved to be of a fine and workable quality. Following the local practice, Jewell split the stones as they lay in the field. During the fall, he drilled holes along the grain to permit water to enter. In winter, the water froze, and by spring, the stone was nearly split apart.

In his record book, Jewell made a double entry for 9 June 1795:

> Deliv^d By Way of John footman one of my gundelo loads of abutments Rocks to George Longe and met with some Diffelty abought them and quite carring.
>
> agreed with Capt. John Salter to carry him a good load of underpinning Stons @ 12 Dollers cash with one month have Don it.[74]

Cargoes of stone were part of the gundalow freighting business into the nineteenth century. William Chase, a prominent Portsmouth resident with mercantile and shipping interests, paid a bill to the "proprietors of Central Wharf Dr. [Dover ?]" on 24 May 1824 "For Wharfage of Gundola Load Stone,

$$\begin{array}{r} \$1.00 \\ \text{Deduct} \quad .50 \\ \hline \$ \ .50^{75} \end{array}$$

Chase's records show he owned a brig, *Mary*, and two ships, *Florenzo* and *Montgomery*. His shipping interests extended as far as the West Indies, the Mississippi, New Orleans and Batavia in the East Indies. Upon receiving his goods from these faraway places, he employed his gundalows to disperse them to the inland ports.

The commercial papers of George Frost shed great light on the role of a typical merchant of his day. (Frost may have inherited his business acumen from his father, also a shrewd merchant; in 1765, the elder Frost exchanged a cow worth seventy pounds with Richard Tucker for a "gundilo" and its delivery to Frost's Wharf at Little Harbor, Portsmouth.) George Frost, a resident of Durham, was active in business from 1795 to 1830, and represents the proverbial "Yankee trader." In his "wood and gondola books," Frost displays his thorough involvement in the building, renting, and hiring of gundalows. The names of two of his gundalows were the *Royal George* and *Old Pinkham*. Two sample entries note: "February 8, 1819, gondolas out---warm as May" ; "December 7, 1819, gondola left at Portsmouth, returned April, 1820." In addition to his gundalows, he owned barns, sheds, and wharves.[76]

Frost linked the New Hampshire hinterland and the coast. He was heavily involved in the lumber business and supplied wood for his Portsmouth customers. In 1806, for example, John Langdon, a wealthy merchant and Governor of the state at that time, who after his Fort William and Mary exploits built an even more magnificent mansion than John Wentworth ever had, was one of Frost's customers. Langdon "offered to buy shook (sets of staves) in return for corn at $.80, rice at $5.75 and flour at $9.00." Other Portsmouth businessmen in return for boards, offered molasses and bakery products. Suppliers of lumber to George Frost lived west of the Great Bay in the villages of Epsom, Northwood and Barnstead. In addition to boards, they supplied finished wood products such as shooks, staves, and shingles. What they wanted in return in addition to fish and salt were the products Frost was obtaining from Portsmouth, so-called West Indies or English goods, commodities such as "three-fourths ton of plaster of Paris, one-half chest of Louchong tea, and three bars of iron."

Gundalow being loaded with cordwood just below the Stratham drawbridge about 1900. A steam tug, which helped displace the gundalow from Piscataqua waters, under power in left background. Eugene Horne photo. PM.

Dealing in cordwood was a specialty of Frost and those relatives who followed him into the business. One of his largest buyers of fire wood was Fort Constitution (the new name for the old fort at New Castle). With records of purchases from 1809 to 1859, Fort Constitution was an especially long-term and lucrative account. Frost entered into an agreement in 1809 to supply oak, maple and birch for that year at $4.00 a cord, plus five shillings a cord for freighting. During Durham's greatest period as a port, from about 1785 to 1830, George Frost, with accounts such as these, was the town's leading merchant.[77]

Another interesting account concerning the wood trade further substantiates John Langdon's heavy involvement in such maters. On 11 November, 1805 William Chase's running account with Langdon lists: "To wharfage 1 gundola load wood," with a charge of $3.70, which Langdon paid in April, 1806.[78]

After an era of building with wood, and being subjected to many terrible fires, Piscataqua citizens sought a safer material. They did not have to look very far. The discovery that the blue clay, packed in natural banks around Great Bay and around the mouths of its rivers, was particularly suited for brickmaking brought a new era for the gundalows. During their heyday, there were at least 43 brickyards in the Piscataqua area, with the greatest concentration of yards at Dover Point. Statistics and dates are few, but the zenith of the brickmaking industry

The Fanny M., *with a full load of brick, passing Split Rock on the Lamprey River, Newmarket about 1890. Note gundalow warehouse on right. Daniel Hedden photo. NHS.*

appears to have come in the 1880s and 1890s. The yards burned twenty to thirty thousand cords of wood a year, which represented many gundalow loads.[79] The Pinkham brickyards at Dover Point and the Henry Abbott brickyards at Sturgeon Creek, Eliot, were huge operations.[80]

Old timers proclaim that the Dover Point brick was the best in New England. In addition to much local use in the construction of mills, factories, and breweries, these bricks found a market throughout New England. Gundalows brought them downstream to Portsmouth and then trans-shipped to Boston. There the bricks were soon transformed into the buildings of Newspaper Row. Many homes on Beacon Hill and the Fens section of that city were built of the superior Dover Point brick. What these two aristocratic neighborhoods gained in the form of fine homes was Piscataqua Bay's loss. So many waterside clay banks were mined that the deposits became exhausted, closing down the brickyards and altering the contours of the shoreline in the process. Now eighty years later, many Beacon Hill and Back Bay residents, cognizant of the building materials used in their homes, "are interested in the construction of the new gundalow, and are donating money for its completion."[81]

During the industrialization of New England, bricks quickly replaced wood. The red brick mill became the dominant feature on the Piscataqua landscape, obscuring the gray, weather beaten fishing shanty, barn and boatyard. These long, low buildings hummed with cotton spindles. Once the raw cotton arrived at Portsmouth, gundalows moved it up to the great mills of Dover, Newmarket and Exeter. Coal and water power made the factories run, tended first by Yankee hands, and later supplemented by waves of immigrants.

Cotton and coal, inexorably linked in this new enterprise, kept the gundalows handsomely employed. From 1815 until the coming of the railroads in 1841 ten Dover-based gundalows were always busy. With the schooners, they moved annually $750,000 worth of goods for the Cocheco Manufacturing Company, a huge textile concern. Half the cotton and all the coal which came to Portsmouth was freighted upstream by gundalows. In 1842 the value of all the goods transported in the back and forth Dover and Portsmouth runs, most of it gundalow-borne, amounted to "two millions, four hundred thousand dollars annually."[82]

With the coming of the winter, gundalows were making their last runs before the river froze. The mills needed adequate stockpiles of cord wood, brick, coal and cotton to last them through the winter months. Many people living near the river's banks made it their business to find temporary work "to assist in unloading these gondolas at the wharves of Portsmouth; for which they were liberally paid in wood. Thus a good supply of fuel was obtained for the coming winter." It was a lively scene at the riverfront as boys boarded a favorite craft to "secure the patronage of a liberal gondola-man."[83]

The Gundalow Ports

Depending upon the gundalows for the shipping and receiving of their cargoes, six Piscataqua towns, Exeter, Newmarket, Durham, Dover, South Berwick and Portsmouth, outgrew their fishing and agricultural origins. The shipbuilding industry and the ship and packet lines, which flourished throughout the Piscataqua Basin, needed as a direct corollary the support of gundalows to sustain their many activities. To varying degrees, depending on their location, waterpower and ultimately their relationship to the railroads, most of these communities prospered with the coming of the industrial age.

*Exeter waterfront on the Squamscott River about 1900, with gundalow docked at
warehouse. Ben's Foto Shop collection. EHS.*

This empire contained some of the largest mills of their kind in
the world. Inventions and technical processes continued the traditional
spirit of innovation of the early Yankee tinker, who was replicated by
thousands of workers, machinists and engineers, backed by local and
Boston capitalists. The busiest place of every community was its landing, complete with cargoes, passengers, wharves, warehouses, gundalows and schooners, with the commercial district extending away from
it. That was the place to go for mail, business or the latest gossip.

Founded in 1638, Exeter grew around the falls of the Squamscott
and Little Rivers where they cascade down to Great Bay. Touring as the
President of the United States in 1789 on a visit, George Washington
noted in his diary these falls "which supply several grist mills, 2 oyle
mills, a slitting mill, and snuff mill." In 1824, Dr. William Perry built a
mill "for the manufacture of starch from potatoes." Convinced that British gum, used by the cotton manufacturers as a sizing for their cloth,
was nothing but charred starch, Perry developed this new and cheaper

Newmarket waterfront on the Lamprey River in the 1890s, showing mills and factories. Note brailed slung yard of gundalow docked at warehouse. Daniel Hedden photo. NHS.

method which supplanted the gum starch. Within a short time, competitors copied Perry's techniques and drove his pioneering mill out of business. Since 1830, the Exeter Manufacturing Company has produced cotton sheeting. At one time the leather tanning industry was so large that Exeter "was the leading manufacturer of saddles throughout the Eastern states."[84]

In addition to producing ships, textiles and shoes, Exeter has been a producer of educated minds for the nation. Founded by John Phillips in 1781 with the granting of a state charter, Phillips Exeter Academy has not forgotten the town's waterfront past. The crew house with its racing shells graces the shoreline of the Squamscott River.

The town of Newmarket, north of Exeter, was another major gundalow port. At the falls of the Lamprey River, Newmarket passed through its initial King's mast, sawmill and grist mill stages to emerge as an industrial community. Founded in 1823, the Newmarket Manufacturing Company became the largest of a number of shoe factories and cotton mills. During the latter half of the nineteenth century, these mills produced annually 7,500,000 yards of cotton cloth.

Gundalow laden with cordwood at the Town Landing, Oyster River, Durham about 1913. PM.

Gundalows carried approximately one half of the cotton and coal for this manufacturing operation. On their approach to the town landing, gundalow captains navigated past land and water signals of danger or safety: the Drifting Elms, Sunken Ledge, High Point Ledge, the Sukey, Coy Rocks, Jimmy Nick's Rock and finally Bear's Garden. Near Shackford's Point the loaded gundalow usually picked up a tug to pull it along to the Newmarket Landing, close by Split Rock. At the "waterside were storehouses having projections overhanging the tide and especially adapted for handling water-borne cargoes." Before the advent of the railroad, gundalows carried most of the freight of the Newmarket Manufacturing Company. At one time the fare between Newmarket and Portsmouth was 12½ cents.[85]

Continuing north along Great Bay and into Little Bay one encounters the Oyster River, so called from "the abundance of oysters found at its mouth." At the head of the tidewater, a group of settlers landed in 1635. Incorporated as Durham in 1732, this town has never industrialized as much as other Piscataqua communities. Farmers grew hay, shipped it to Portsmouth and eventually raised it for the Boston market. Ledges of Exeter diorite, found in Durham, proved to be another source of profit. After shearing off the exposed ledges, the farmers shipped these "Durham flagstones" to Portsmouth for use in stone walks. Undoubtedly Captain Marshall Jewell's fieldstones were originally part of these ledges. Later generations had to work a little harder for the stones.

After the Revolutionary War, "the town lapsed into rural quiet." The town revived with the establishment of the State College of Agriculture and the Mechanic Arts in 1893, from which emerged the University of New Hampshire. Except for the Saturday afternoon football clashes on Lewis Fields and occasional exuberant fraternity parties to celebrate a victory or to drown sorrows over defeat, Durham has retained its quieter ways.

The shallowness of the Oyster River undoubtedly contributed to Durham's escape from the mixed blessing of industrialization. The river could not support the volume of traffic needed for such mills. Even to this day, a pilot is cautioned, for safety's sake, to navigate upstream to the site of the landing. The town, nevertheless, recognizes and honors its legacy from the gundalow years. In 1974, the town selectmen adopted a town seal depicting a gundalow under sail with a rising sun in the background, quite as one might have viewed this scene from the Falls Bridge two centuries before. This seal graces the sign in front of the Town Offices, located near the falls of Oyster River.[86]

Dover, bounded by four tidewater rivers, was, perhaps, the center of gundalow activity of the inland ports. The settlement of Dover Point in 1623 justifies its claim to be the oldest continuously occupied settlement in the state. Dropping some thirty-three feet in the center of the city, Cocheco Falls has supplied water power to turn the wheels of industry since Richard Waldron built a mill here in 1642. The Cocheco Manufacturing Company, incorporated in 1827, dominated the town's economy for almost one hundred years. Successive waves of immigrant groups tended its cotton looms. The company also printed calico. Other Dover industries, during the 1850s, included a carpet factory, a machine shop for the manufacture of railroad cars and two flannel producing plants. Before the railroads pre-empted their business gundalows were Dover's lifeline to other ports, and maintained Dover's position as the crossroads of the Piscataqua.[87]

"Dover Landing." View of the mills of the Cocheco Manufacturing Company at the falls of the Cocheco River. Oil painting by William Stoodley Gookin (1799–c. 1872). GB.

At the mouth of the Cocheco River, gundalowmen could either follow the Piscataqua fourteen miles to the sea, or turn north (or portside) to the Salmon Falls River, known to the Indians as the Newichawannock ("Wigwam Place") River. Heading northward up the Salmon Falls River, the watery boundary between Maine and New Hampshire, they would ultimately arrive at a sheltered anchorage off Pipestave Falls. Rollinsford is on the New Hampshire side; South Berwick is situated on the opposite bank, some sixteen miles upriver from New Castle.

The early history of South Berwick follows a familiar pattern of ample water power, vast areas of timber, the establishment of mills, landings and gundalow service. About 1623, Ambrose Gibbons erected a mill, perhaps the first in America. Later cotton and woolen mills followed, taking advantage of the water power generated by the Lower and Upper Falls. From the countryside, ponderous oxen hauled their loads of lumber to the Lower Landing. At the landing gundalows picked up the timber and delivered it to the Navy Yard. In 1854, "there were still twenty gundalows sailing from the Landing wharves," wrote Sarah

Gundalows docked at Kittery Point, Maine, with Lady Pepperrell House in the background. DAC.

Orne Jewett, a lifelong native of South Berwick and the granddaughter of a local shipbuilder.[88]

To this day the "Counting House" stands close by the Falls. Built between 1827 and 1830, this brick structure was the financial center of the activities of the Portsmouth Manufacturing Company, a cotton manufacturer. On the first floor, it housed "the offices, the sales room, the records, [and] the offices of the officials." A ballroom was on the second floor. A dance, the "Lighting-Up Ball," sponsored by the company, was the social event of the year. Held usually in October, this dance issued invitations which "were prized beyond rubies." Now this building houses the Old Berwick Historical Society.[89]

Also contributing to the brisk business of the gundalow captains were the cotton and woolen mills of the Salmon Falls Manufacturing Company at Salmon Falls, the industrial section of Rollinsford.[90]

As "All roads lead to Rome," all waters eventually lead to Portsmouth, "the Queen of the Piscataqua," where sooner or later all gundalows docked, and their captains and crews walked along Market Street, the location of the wharves and warehouses.

"Church Point" (1884), Portsmouth, with gundalows both docked and underway on the Piscataqua. Ink drawing by Abbott F. Graves. From Albee's New Castle.

Portsmouth has supported itself with many diverse activities. When one economy declined, another rose to take its place, adjusting to the times. After its initial fishing and mast pine days, the town flourished following the American Revolution. Exemplifying the symbol of a ship on the state seal, Portsmouth has relied upon some type of a ship to maintain its vitality, whether a schooner sailing to the West Indies, a warship being built at the Navy Yard, a clipper ship breezing ahead across the Atlantic, a lobster boat stopping to pull up its pots or an excursion boat taking tourists out to the Isles of Shoals. For most of its history, until the twentieth century, the gundalow worked in tandem with this maritime economy as the cargo-freight boats of their day.

The Portsmouth Naval Shipyard, founded in 1800, has built warships and enriched Portsmouth throughout this long association. The lucrative West Indian trade in the 1700s and early 1800s exported pine boards and planks, dried fish and beef, and the ships returned home with molasses, rum, sugar and cocoa. These profits built the fine homes along Middle Street. Wealthy merchants cultivated the arts. During the

War of 1812, Portsmouth captains turned to privateering. After that conflict, Portsmouth resumed its shipbuilding and fishing, and engaged in a little whaling. But the flush times of the West Indian trade did not fully return. Part of this decline was reversed by the California gold rush, and the demand for fast and large ships. Between 1840 and 1860, 169 vessels were built in the District of Portsmouth, including twenty-eight clipper ships.

In his classic boy's novel, *The Story of a Bad Boy* (1869), Thomas Bailey Aldrich referred to the overall post-War of 1812 decline in the fortunes of "Rivermouth," the fictional name he used for his native town, writing:

> Few ships come to Rivermouth now. Commerce drifted into other ports. The phantom fleet sailed off one day, and never came back again. The crazy old warehouses are empty; and the barnacles and eel-grass cling to the piles of the crumbling wharves....[91]

Set in ante-bellum Portsmouth, Aldrich's novel describes a Portsmouth which had seen better days. With the outbreak of the Civil War, however, the Navy Yard exploded with work, laying keels for Federal warships. With its sons in the Army or Navy, or working at the Yard, a wartime economy gripped the city. After the end of the war in 1865, Portsmouth sought to maintain this prosperity. Handicapped by the lack of waterpower for the operation of large scale cotton and lumber mills, the city turned to other enterprises. Frank Jones (1832–1902), a self-made man almost out of the pages of Charles Dudley Warner and Mark Twain's *The Gilded Age*, stood as a colossus astride the Piscataqua and built breweries, hotels, railroads and button and shoe factories. He put the city back to work. Railroads brought tourism to Portsmouth for the beaches, sea air and historic homes, doubling the town's population during the summer months. The past continues to attract attention. The gundalow replica was built at Strawbery Banke, a historical restoration. The vessel was launched in 1982 near the same Puddle Dock site where its ancestors were picked up by the incoming Piscataqua tide 350 years ago.

The Captains and Crews of the Gundalows

Gundalowmen were a special breed. Like Western cowboys, Mississippi River steamboat pilots, and Maine hunting and fishing guides, they

REGULAR LINE OF
PACKETS
Between Dover & Portsmouth.

THE subscriber having purchased of *Stephen Twombly* his BOATS, which said Twombly has run between Dover and Portsmouth, would now say to the public, that he has commenced running a REGULAR LINE OF BOATS between DOVER and PORTSMOUTH, for the purpose of transporting Merchandise, Lumber, &c. consisting of the Sloop WASHINGTON and the Packet MENTOR; and also a supply of GONDOLAS when occasion requires. The subscriber having been engaged for several years in the coasting business between Dover and Boston, flatters himself that he can do the Freigting business between Dover and Portsmouth, in a manner that will be satisfactory to those who may employ him, and solicits a share of patronage.

All orders left with Andrew Peirce, Jr. or Andrew Peirce, Jr. & Son, will receive prompt attention, and satisfaction given or no pay

JAMES WENTWORTH.

N. B. Smallest favors gratefully received.
March 19, 1842.   1S

An 1842 newspaper advertisement or broadside of James Wentworth, offering packet and gundalow service between Dover and Portsmouth. Note that Wentworth bought out Stephen Twombly, noted Dover gundalowman. UNHMS photo. RWC.

lived by their own rules, respected no one, and relished their independence. Colorful characters, they were superstitious — and experts in swearing and drinking. In 1812 Captain Mark Grant of South Berwick saw a falling star while navigating his gundalow on the Piscataqua. Everyone aboard stopped and was frightened. Undoubtedly, after a quick drink, they were on their way again.

All accounts agree that these river men loved their work, "going gundalowing," with a sense of freedom on the water.

During their own times, the gundalowmen were regarded as pariahs in the nautical caste system. Their lot was to perform rough and heavy service, with little romance or reward. Blue water sailors treated with contempt anyone associated with "square toed frigates," or "Portsmouth pleasure boats," as gundalows were often called. Captain Johnson Stevens of the schooner *Sally*, out of Kennebunk, Maine, sneered, "A Man that would sail a gundilo would Rob the Church Yard."[92]

We know little of the early gundalow captains except their names. The skippers of record on the Dover to Portsmouth run during the first half of the nineteenth century include Moses Young, John Sayles, James Dame, Benjamin Ford, Stephen Twombly and Enoch Dunn. Captain Joseph Fernald of Exeter began his career in 1817 and wore out three gundalows during his lifetime. When Fernald died in 1848 his son George carried on the family tradition. Plying his gundalows, *Dido*, *News-Letter*, *Redjacket* and *Alice* on the rivers he must have known as a boy at his father's side, he followed his calling until his death in 1900. Once in May, 1876, heavily loaded "with a cargo of lime, cement, laths, and plaster" for Portsmouth, he returned with "one-hundred and five hogshead of salt for the fishermen on the Squamscot." Heavy seas racked his gundalow, *Alice*, on this trip but she weathered the elements without incident. "Seasickness," a reporter noted, "was scarcely heard of among the crew."[93]

As the gundalow era drew toward its end, several captains achieved fame, if not notoriety, on the river. Captain Harry Watson, piloting the *Fearless*, was acknowledged as one of the best, with his skills frequently improved with drams of rum. Captain Hypie (or Hype) Philpot of Salmon Falls was one of a kind. A very large and dark man, Hypie was a superb pilot, "half slammed" or not, according to one who remembered him. To test his new deckhands, Hypie would throw them overboard to see if they could swim. One man could not, and drowned. Despite his wild ways, Philpot was an innovator and once owned a steam gundalow. But his experiment was impractical because the eel grass in the river clogged the gundalow's engine. Eventually Philpot was shot dead in a Dover tavern.[94]

Gooch Cheney of South Berwick also represented the rough-and-tumble school of gundalow captains. His son Jocum and Al Boucher made up his crew on runs to Portsmouth with a load of brick or wood. Telling his crew to have salt pork and potatoes for supper when they arrived in Portsmouth, Old Gooch would invariably disappear. After two or three instances of this behavior, the boys decided to follow him. Tailing the old man from a safe distance, they discovered that he entered a restaurant for a hearty meal. His son was so angry that he wanted to hang Gooch on the spot.

Their exploits and customs live on, half in legend, one quarter in fact, and another quarter in downright deliberate falsehood. Stories and anecdotes about them abound, since they were natural storytellers. Without these items of folklore part of the spirit and mystique of gundalowing would be lost. One doesn't expect total accuracy. Through these stories, soon becoming fish stories with successive tellings, we can see the gundalowmen in their special world.

Stories kept tumbling out of the mouths of the men on the river, true and not. A certain gundalow captain always kept a keg of rum hidden for his use on one of the islands. When he arrived at anchorage, he sent his mate ashore for a pint of rum from the keg. At that moment the yard knocked the captain overboard, and as he came up he hollered, "Bill, bring a quart."[95]

Captain Young of Dover passed into legend with his mad exploit. On occasion with perfect weather conditions, gundalows would go to Boston or to Cape Cod with a load of brick, returning with marsh hay. But Young was unimpressed with these short runs. In 1888, he rigged up his gundalow with a schooner sail and started down the Atlantic coast. One of the booms hit one of his crew, who "was lost overboard." Upon arriving at Galveston, Texas, the captain's luck ran out. A storm and tidal wave hit at that moment, and the flood washed his gundalow two miles inland, dropping his craft next to a church.[96]

The brickyard workers and the bridge toll takers, which gundalowmen usually became for their declining years, were also stalwarts in this river society. Dover Point seemed to breed a certain type. George Ford was a brickmaker there and once asked his nephews for a bird for supper. He promised to cook it for them. After the boys fetched a turkey, George covered it with clay and cooked it in a kiln. They ate it that afternoon. Upon learning that they had taken one of his turkeys, George Ford was tearing mad.

"Uncle George," they responded, "you were willing to eat the other fellow's turkey."

Working around the brickyard in his bare feet, George Ford would walk in tar and then sand "to give his feet a good tough bottom." To make a little extra money, he would approach passersby and "for two pence would walk across the hot kiln of brick." Ford's eccentricity was inherited from his father whose name is lost to history. A hermit and "a tough old man," the father's job was to block up gundalows and caulk the seams when necessary. Once a gundalow fell off its blocking, landing on top of him. After two tides, some men found him and pulled out the old geezer unhurt.[97]

To maintain such remarkable constitutions, the gundalowmen obviously possessed some secrets. To cure asthma, they would boil potato peelings and then drink the water. Boils presented no problem. The remedy for that ailment was to "Put one teaspoonful of lead shot into a glass of water. Put in back of stove and keep lukewarm for 5 Hours. Then drink water."

Gundalowmen also had definite ideas about food. One captain said that a compass wasn't much good and that he would rather have a potato. "A compass couldn't tell you where you were," he said, "but a potato could be eaten if you were hungry." To the culinary world, the gundalowmen contributed a new recipe, "Spit in the Eye." One took a "large piece of homemade bread, cut a hole in the center, butter it well, put an egg in the center, and put it in the oven to bake."[98]

The early gundalow ferry operators often contended with much more than tricky tides. Before the Piscataqua Bridge was built in 1794, John Knight conducted his ferry business from Brown's Camp to Fox Point across Little Bay. His wife, Sally, "was believed to be a witch and had very black eyes." When it was time to kill a pig, Sally told her husband, "Stay thy hand, John, until the tide and moon are right or the pork will shrink in the pot." Then she would check her almanac and calculate the right time and tide for the pig's execution. After John's death she was seen walking along the Piscataqua Road, sputtering and swearing because John was so comfortable in his grave, and she was walking the road.[99]

A gundalow-related story, catching the earthy humor of those days, has been preserved by Robert Whitehouse, who relates:

Captain [James H.] Card lived down at Dover Point. To picture the area, you have to realize that he was not right on the point, but inland a bit, such as it was, and he had a bull and perhaps a cow or two. Down the road towards Portsmouth was the Dover Point Bridge. This was a draw-bridge. When the gundalows and boats wanted to go through, they'd get out the fish horn and blow the horn to open the draw. Well, Captain Card had this bull that had become sick, and he decided to straighten it out and give him an enema. He couldn't think how to get this into the old bull, so he happened to look around, and saw the old fish horn. He took some turpentine and whatever else you mix up to put in the bull and he stuck this horn in the back of the bull and he poured this in. Well, I suppose circumstance, and the old bull didn't feel too good. He ramped and raged around, and broke loose. Started down the road. Hadn't gone very far when that horn let out a blast. The old bridge keeper heard the noise, so he looked upriver and downriver and didn't see a gundalow or vessel coming, but thought, well, must be pretty near, to make a noise like that, and he went out on the bridge and got the turning tool, and put it in the center and opened up the bridge. In a few seconds another blast, and he says, by golly, that boat is coming pretty fast. It wasn't long before the bull got to the bridge. Just ran right out on the bridge and ran right off and in the river and was drowned. That's a true story.[100]

As late as 1891, the draw bridge at Dover Point was opened 924 times during the year, allowing 1,266 vessels, including 495 gundalows, to pass through. Jim Drew was the toll taker during the day, Jim Card of runaway bull fame worked evenings, and Ben Butler handled occasional nights. Butler also owned his own gundalow, appropriately named *Ben Butler* after himself. Others in his fleet included the *Edgar Weston*, *Tiller* and *Paul*. Born to the river life, Butler represented a typical second-generation figure to the profession. His father was a river pilot, guiding schooners to Exeter and back to Portsmouth. His charge was ten dollars each way. Once a schooner captain decided to save the pilot charge. While rounding Bloody Point, his vessel grounded on the rocks. The ship was a total loss. Its skeleton remained on the rocks for many years, serving as a graphic reminder to any niggardly schooner captain the advisability of employing a qualified pilot. The wrecked ship was free advertising for pilot service.[101]

Decline and Demise of the Gundalows

"They were tough buggers, those gundalows," remembered an old Portsmouth resident. During the last half of the nineteenth century, railroads, bridges, and steam-powered tugs increasingly pre-empted the gundalow, but tough, defiant and antiquated, it lingered on. Toward the end of the decade, 1890–1900, the few remaining gundalows, which owed their longevity to sentiment more than to anything else, gradually disappeared from the Piscataqua. Like dinosaurs in their death throes, these last gundalows were rotting away "their timbers on the mud-banks of the Piscataqua River about 1900." There was no newspaper reporter or photographer to record the scene; the gundalow slipped away as quietly and as unnoticed as the phantom fleet of Thomas Bailey Aldrich's "Rivermouth." No one mourned its passing. The Piscataqua River gundalow died of old age, about 250 years after it was born.[102]

The more the fortunes of the railroad rose, accelerating more rapidly toward the end of the century, the quicker the gundalow declined. Locked in an almost Darwinian struggle for survival, the railroads and gundalows fought a seventy-year battle. This saga began in 1835, when the Boston and Maine Railroad, with its headquarters in Boston, was chartered in New Hampshire. As the railroad headed northward, it swept away all opposition.

By 1838, the Boston and Maine reached Haverhill, Massachusetts; during that same year, its roar was figuratively heard across the border in Dover, New Hampshire. The town had a mass meeting and wanted the line so badly that many of its citizens subscribed for stock. The railhead reached Exeter in June, 1840, generating a tremendous interest, with spectators watching the laying of the tracks. The survey lines pointed north. Aiding in their own eventual downfall, gundalows and schooners arrived at the Newfields and Newmarket Landings with iron rails and other supplies. At no time in their history was the activity at these landings more hectic. During the summer of 1841, the railroad extended its lines through Newmarket, Durham and Dover. In 1849, the Concord and Portsmouth Railroad, skirting Great Bay, joined at the Newmarket-Newfields track to form a rail junction. The road was completed to Concord in 1852. The railroad not only took the gundalow's cargoes and routes, but also operated year-round. With a little shoveling to clear the tracks after a snow storm, the railroad continued its regular service. As the locomotive sped by, the gundalow, with the bays frozen for three months, was laying idly on shore, losing business.[103]

No gundalow port suffered more than Durham. In laying its lines from Newmarket to Dover in 1841, the Boston and Maine surveyors and track-laying crews bypassed the business district around the landing. The tracks were located on the western edge of the township to assure a relatively straight and economically feasible route to Dover. Two stage lines, operating from Dover to Boston since 1812, stopped at the Durham stage depot, one running by the way of Haverhill and the other through Newburyport. With the arrival of the railroad, the stage lines immediately went out of business. The iron horse could outrun its living counterpart. Soon Durham village became a quiet place, "delightful for residence, but not for business." The gundalows, which for years had conveyed loads of cordwood from the Oyster River Landing to Portsmouth, made fewer and fewer voyages, and finally business ceased. Also contributing to this transition, the Durham farmers now realized a better price selling their wood to the railroad.[104]

The railroad's impact upon Dover was enormous. Once the Boston and Maine reached Dover in 1841, the railroad altered the entire commercial activity of the town. The landing at Cocheco Falls had been the center of business, with the schooners and gundalows discharging and taking on cargoes at the wharves on the river. The Dover-Packet Company soon discharged its last cargo. Business was now diverted about a half mile north to upper Central Avenue "around the railroad station and the streets leading to it." The iron horse kept charging ahead, hitching Dover's future to it. By the end of 1842, the Boston and Maine line reached its junction point with the Portland, Saco and Portsmouth at South Berwick, Maine, across the Salmon Falls River. The connection went into use in February, 1843. Tapping the Lake Winnipesaukee trade, the Cocheco Railroad linked Dover with Alton in 1850. While the railroad brought new industries to Dover and increased local trade, the town's importance as a distributing point for interior trade declined. Losers in this transportation revolution were gundalows, stagecoach lines, wayside coach inns and taverns, and oxen teams.[105]

Railroad fever continued unabated. The Eastern Railroad, another Massachusetts company, eyed Portsmouth. Chartered in 1836, the line wasted no time, extending from Boston northward to Salem in 1838, to Newburyport by 28 August 1840, to the New Hampshire state line by November 9 and to Portsmouth itself by December 31. The fare from East Boston to Portsmouth, a distance of 54 miles, was $2.00 — nearly four cents a mile. At Portsmouth the Eastern Railroad connected with steamers that ran to Portland, but that arrangement was short-lived.[106]

Approaching Portsmouth from the opposite direction, the Portland, Saco & Portsmouth Railroad pushed south from the Maine metropolis. Passing through Kennebunk, North and South Berwick and Kittery, the company built the 52-mile line in about a year and a half. Constructing a bridge across the Piscataqua, which took advantage of Nobles Island in the river, the railroad made its connection to Portsmouth in 1842. Its effect upon Portsmouth was immediate. No longer did the steamers make runs between Portsmouth and Portland; the railroad absorbed that business. Moreover, the Portsmouth Bridge, as it was called, served a dual purpose. Its builders constructed a wagon-way for the use of wagons, horses and pedestrians. Charles W. Brewster's 1850 map of Portsmouth clearly shows this phenomenon with a "Toll House" and "Timber Dock" on Nobles Island. The typical New England railroad bridge of the nineteenth century was a "two-story affair, the upper level carrying the railroad track, the lower the wagon-way, which the railroad was to keep in repair." The Portsmouth Bridge may have been of this design or, perhaps, two parallel spans on the same level. At any rate, the ferry boat and the gundalow captains saw their livelihoods reduced.[107]

The iron ring around the Piscataqua Basin was completed and welded together during the short span of four years (1840–1843). All six gundalow ports were now served by rail lines. The next and ultimately finishing blow to the Piscataqua gundalows was delayed until the 1870s. The iron circle was about to be bisected, with a railroad bridge spanning the Piscataqua at Dover Point. As early as 1842 the Portsmouth & Dover Railroad was chartered as a corporation, but its officers could not raise the capital to begin construction. In 1872 Frank Jones became president and directed his attention to bringing direct rail service to these two cities. The old Piscataqua Bridge had been carried away by the ice on 18 February 1855, and its owners could not afford to repair it. The nearby railroads had diverted much of its former traffic anyway. By the 1870s the existing ferry service at Dover Point across Little Bay could not effectively cope with transportation needs.

Jones let nothing stop him. Difficult engineering problems did not faze him. Discovering that it would be necessary to have a truss at the eastern end of the planned 1880-foot bridge, Jones traveled to Chicago in 1873 to buy a Howe truss for that span. The work was completed on both the railroad and highway sections late in 1873. On 9 February 1874 the first train ran between Portsmouth and Dover. Wagons paid a toll to cross.

Derelict gundalow, Paul Jones, *built and piloted by Jeremiah Paul, rotting away at Eliot Bridge near the confluence of Piscataqua River and Quamphegan Brook about 1905. Only the knees and bottom beams and timbers remain. Built at Rollinsford in 1867, the* Paul Jones *was 60.3 feet long, and named for the Revolutionary War naval hero. UNHMS.*

With the completion of this bridge the gundalows faced not only a further reduction in their business but also a navigational hazard. Gundalows always hugged the east — or Newington — side of the bridge, with the "Horse Races" just ahead. At least one gundalow loaded with bricks was carried into the bridge pilings and capsized. Its cargo of undelivered bricks remains at the bottom of the Piscataqua to this day, observed by divers who are content to let them rest there.

In time, motor trucks and automobiles used the wagon road section of the bridge. Well built to withstand the rigors of winter ice, this structure provided service until 1934, when it was replaced by the new General John Sullivan Bridge.[108]

The decade of the seventies brought still another blow to the gundalows. In 1870 the steam tug *Clara Bateman* was brought to Portsmouth. Built in 1863 at Lamberton, New Jersey, this boat was 65-feet long, registered forty tons and had fifty horsepower. Although tugs had sporadically appeared on the Piscataqua as early as 1850 in connection with the California trade, the *Clara Bateman* was the first

Wreck of the Fanny M. *at Dover Point in 1925, showing the loss of her leeboard. Cutwater and remains of the windlass on left, with cuddy on right. A. V. de Forest photo. UNHMS.*

tug ever owned in the region and regularly employed on the river. Captain Albert Rand operated the *Bateman* on the local waters for twenty years with little competition until larger and more powerful boats crowded her out.[109]

The era of the gundalows was over. Newer, faster and year-round forms of transportation criss-crossed their old domain. The end could not long be delayed. According to Captain Edward H. Adams, "The last gundalow out of Durham River left in August 1889 with a load of bricks for Portsmouth Navy Yard." After 1900, Adams's *Fanny M.* was the only gundalow in operation, hauling coal to Exeter and supplies to Newmarket. At the end of her days, Captain Frank Coleman of Dover Point skippered the *Fanny M.* in freighting materials for the brick-yards. On his property, Coleman beached her for the last time, and the hull lay there for years, rotting away as a derelict in the sun and rain.

In the winter of 1930 or 1931, her long abandoned hull finally broke up in the ice and disappeared. The last operating gundalow on the Piscataqua had taken her final voyage.[110]

Captain Edward Hamlin Adams (1860–1951), last of the gundalow builders and pilots, in his ninetieth year. Douglas Armsden photo. DAC.

II *Captain Edward H. Adams, the Last of the Gundalowmen*

The Homestead at Adams Point

AS THE BUILDER, OWNER AND PILOT of the *Fanny M.*, the last working gundalow on the Piscataqua, Captain Edward H. Adams was the last active gundalowman. Adams kept the tradition of his profession alive through his personality, interviews with boating enthusiasts, and building gundalow models. He lived through and witnessed the transition of the Piscataqua region from the era of the gundalow with teams of oxen and block ice cutting during the winter to a new age which brought speed boats and oil spills polluting the river. During his last years, as he viewed the full sweep of Great Bay from his lifelong home at Adams Point, the old captain remembered earlier days when twenty-five boats of various types would pass by his house at one time. "The traffic is all overhead now," he remarked sadly.[1]

For many years, Adams Point has survived as a pastoral refuge in the midst of an increasingly industrialized landscape. Once an island, Adams Point was long ago connected to the mainland by a causeway. The point of land, originally called Matthews Neck, is magnificently situated on the Durham shore at the Narrows between Great and Little Bays. In the spring, green fields speckled with dandelions meet the river and the marsh grass. Tall oaks and elms reach skyward against a backdrop of evergreens. Black mallards, geese, and other game birds feed on the marshes. Deer winter here.

"Reformation" John Adams, the captain's grandfather, obtained this eighty-acre tract in 1830. A Methodist minister of Newington, he served God and himself in a fortuitous business deal with Timothy Dame of Durham to resolve a $500.00 debt. The good minister, holding a

"Portrait of 'Reformation' John Adams," owner and patriarch of Adams Point. Oil painting by Jeremiah Pease. GB.

"The Adams House and Cove from Shooting Point," oil painting by Olive Esther Libbey Adams (1840–1931), mother of Captain Adams. GB.

mortgage on this land as security for the loan, acquired the property through Dame's default. This land remained in the hands of successive generations of the Adams family until 1961. "Reformation" John had served his descendants well by providing the ancestral homestead; his shrewdness in business affairs quickly earned him another nickname, "Speculation" John. This tract of land became known as Adams Point.[2]

"Reformation" John also left his family a good name. John's father was the Rev. Joseph Adams of Newington. He was an uncle of John Adams, the young lawyer who used the Piscataqua ferries in 1770 en route, eventually, to the Presidency. A cherished memento in "Reformation" John Adams' home, built in the 1830s with twenty-one rooms, was a replica of the family coat of arms which had originated in Wales in 1190. The motto on the coat of arms, true to the Adams' spirit, reads, "Persevere, Aspire, and Indulge Not!" This approach to life was part of the Adams heritage.[3]

Married in 1820, "Reformation" John fathered six children. A Methodist circuit rider, he died in 1850 at the age of 59. For his interment, the family built the handsome Adams tomb overlooking Great Bay. His youngest son, Joseph Martin Reuter Adams, was content to remain at Adams Point. Joseph's older brothers wandered off. One worked in Kansas as a newspaper correspondent and another fought in the Civil War.

Joseph married Olive Esther Libbey of Berwick, Maine, in 1860. Improving his inherited property, he farmed extensively and owned a brickyard there. He was also a river captain and owned gundalows. Active in community affairs, he was a selectman of Durham in 1887. During the 1880s he and his wife founded the Adams House, a famous summer boardinghouse resort. It was a successful enterprise to which he devoted much attention until his death in 1917.[4]

The Life of Captain Adams

Edward Hamlin Adams, the son of Joseph and Olive Esther, was born on 22 October 1860 at Adams Point. He was the sailor of the family and never wanted to be anything else. Edward was the future heir to a self-sufficient world at Adams Point, a "feudal estate," with the great house, "fine black oxen, milk cows, gardens," complete with outbuildings, including a blacksmith shop. Grandfather John had even provided a Pest House, built during the smallpox epidemics of the early eighteenth century. The main house looked out to Great Bay and a cove formed by a slender arm of land ending at Shooting Point. This sheltered place was a natural harbor. Edward remained here as a country squire throughout his ninety years. Why should he ever want to leave?[5]

His mother was an accomplished artist and Edward inherited her talent. As a boy he began carving ship models, including a coastal schooner. He often visited Newfields (then South Newmarket) and boarded the sailing schooners moored in the Squamscott River. From his house he looked over this watery highway carrying the commerce of the Piscataqua aboard its many vessels.

At the age of twelve the boy almost drowned near his home. On 30 July 1873 a number of Newmarket people boarded a packet — a small passenger boat resembling in many ways a gundalow. The old packet, originally called the *Grey Eagle*, had been idle for years, but was relaunched as the *Factory Girl*. The packet left Newmarket on a pleasure excursion and landed at Adams Point for a picnic lunch. It took no extra coaxing on the part of the packet's captain and passengers for young Edward to join them for a sail after lunch. The old vessel embarked again. As she was entering Little Bay, a sudden squall hit the *Factory Girl*. The boat capsized. "Carelessness and lack of knowledge were the real culprits," Adams later recalled. Not a swimmer, Edward clung to a spar to remain afloat. An older boy fought him for this lifesaving piece of buoyant wood, but Edward beat off his attack. He

"Piscataqua Packet," model made by Captain Adams. This type of vessel, used for passenger service, was eventually deemed unsafe and ceased operations in the 1870s. GB.

and most of the other passengers were rescued by Thomas Robinson and George Savage, standing by in their sailboats. They were the lucky ones. Three young women drowned in this tragedy.

The survivors were taken to the Adams House for dry clothing and hot food. For this act of kindness, the survivors and their families presented the Adams family with a sterling silver serving dish bearing the inscription, "Gratitude July 30, 1873." Thereafter the Adamses used this special dish for afternoon cake. For his part, Edward "learned to swim that very summer."[6]

The packet as a form of passenger transportation ended her days with this accident. Deemed unsafe, the packets disappeared from the river.

Despite this mishap Edward Adams was not dissuaded from a career on the Piscataqua. In 1882 he modelled a gundalow in preparation for building the full scale craft. During the winter of 1882–1883, he selected and cut the principal timbers and logs for his project. The straight pieces he easily obtained from his own woodlot. Finding the crooked pieces for the vessel's knees and bow logs required more time, but it was time pleasantly spent. He was courting Martha Frances Harvey of Red Oak Hill in nearby Epping. Practical as he was, the ardent suitor made every trip count twice. He always looked for knees along the way. In pursuing these double objectives, Edward Adams decided to marry Frances first. On 11 January 1885 they were wed. In 1886 he completed the gundalow, and inverting the names, called her the *Fanny M.* after his wife.[7]

To this union, three children were born. Harvey Thompson, the first child, was born in 1891 but he died that same year. Edward Cass was born in 1892, followed in 1897 by their daughter, Avis Suzanne.

For many years Adams earned his livelihood on the river, gundalowing and boat building. "I had to make a living," he once remarked, "and that's an awful setback to a fellow." He freighted much of the brick to Portsmouth for the building of its schoolhouses and to Dover for the Kennedy block. On one trip, Adams carried sixty tons on the *Fanny M.*, which, in his words, "took some navigatin' between the tide and the wind." So precise was Adams' timing that his wife, Frances, used "to put an apple pie in the oven when she saw the gundalow coming into view from Newmarket Point. By the time the Captain arrived at Adams Point the pie was fully baked and put on a skiff to take to her husband's gundalow on its way to Portsmouth." All who knew him believed Adams had some inherent telepathy with the tides and the

Cass Adams, with his father, Captain Edward H. Adams. UNHMS.

phases of the moon. He knew the river by instinct. It was no wonder he was always known as "the Captain," although Adams never served in any military capacity. Close friends and his son, Cass, however, always called him "the Skipper," as a token of their esteem.[8]

The Captain, whose family had lived on Adams Point for three generations, appeared to have developed a mysterious rapport with the plants and animals there. When the *Fanny M.* entered Great Bay, Captain Adams threw over his anchor, boarded his skiff, and rowed across to Adams Point for a night at home. Occasionally a gauzy fog would settle over the river, but he did not allow this gray mist to bother him. Whenever the fog rolled in one of the Captain's cows "always went to the water's edge and there set up a regular series of blasts that rivalled modern power-driven fog-horns." With this automatic fog-horn bellowing, the Captain easily found his way to shore, tied up his skiff, and headed home across the fields. Adams always paid his respects to his faithful cow.[9]

Adams's longevity may be attributed to his lifelong regimen of hard work and physical activity. About 5 feet 5 inches tall and weighing

110 pounds, he rose at 4:00 A.M. almost every morning to tend to his chores. "We wrecked!" he always exclaimed upon confronting a crisis in his work. Adams then analyzed the problem in silence for a few minutes. "We've got to salvage," he would then say. He never threw anything away. Sooner or later, a piece of wood, rejected for one project, would come in handy for something else. Often he would find a shoe on the shore of Great Bay and would pick it up to save it, in hopes of finding its mate. Frequently he would. Adams lived simply and frugally.

One of the two extant diaries the Captain kept describes his activities during the early 1890s. (The diary is undated by year.) This pencilled record in a lined account book chronicles his steady work habits and the keeping of accurate financial entries. As a conscientious businessman, he kept a record of his income as well as his expenses. He was loading, unloading, gundalowing, cutting and hauling wood, repairing boats, haying, butchering pigs, making models, and occasionally "puttering around."

On May 14 his first entry reads: "Bill carried me to the gunlow at the Mathes place paid Leon Cramma ten Dollars over pa[i]d him." His expenses, incurred over a number of trips, recall the good old days of phonetic spelling and inexpensive prices: "Cloak 10.00; oringes .30; horse put up .50; teeth fixed 1.00; dinner .60; hare cut .25; soda .30; sigars .15; extry help 3.36; canday .05; horse shod .75; pie .10; meat .30; caned stuff 1.00; stockens .15; thimble .05; axle greece .25 and bit .50"[10]

Almost every entry contains a description of the weather, a standard concern of any river pilot or farmer. On rainy or stormy days he and his hired hand attended to indoor work. On May 31 he "went to Portsmouth with the stone got as far as the anchoring ground of Fords and waited till day light and went to the brig [bridge] and got to far out in the tide and had to let go the anchor and waited till the tide slackened and went as far as the elms and I went a shore and walked to Portsmouth." Other crises included a gundalow stuck in the mud on June 5, and a torn sail of his gundalow during October, which he finally had mended in Portsmouth. On November 30—Thanksgiving day, in his diary entry— the Captain must have had a hasty turkey dinner. On that day he blocked up his gundalow for the winter.

On occasional Sundays he would drive Fanny and the baby in the family buggy to Epping for a visit with his inlaws. In rare moments of relaxation, he would go fishing or blueberrying with his hired man. In the late 1890s, he built a sailing sharpie, *Klondike*, for excursions on Great Bay. Adams never seems to have taken a vacation or to have

Adams House and outbuildings, with the Fanny M. *docked in Adams Cove. Anon. collection.*

traveled outside the Piscataqua region. His world was complete with work, friends and hobbies.[11]

In addition to these activities Adams and his father grew tobacco filler on the farm from 1902 to 1908. After the tobacco had been dried they used Havana wrappers for the manufacture of cigars, employing a wooden tobacco press. In 1907 Edward Adams delivered 20,000 unboxed cigars at Durham to a receiver of C. C. Winkley, a Lynn, Massachusetts, tobacconist, paying the Strafford County Deputy Sheriff $4.10 in fees. For the second half of the year 1908, Adams paid his stamp tax on cigars, amounting to $13.30, to the Collector's Office of the United States Internal Revenue at Portsmouth. But this tobacco-growing experiment was abandoned. The Captain was fond of cigars as a younger man and undoubtedly smoked some of his profits before they reached the market. During his last years he enjoyed his pipe, puffing away as he related his endless supply of stories.[12]

With the decline of river traffic on the Piscataqua and the demise of his own *Fanny M.*, Captain Adams devoted his middle years to the family hotel business. For those guests who desired a complete break from twentieth century distractions, the Adams summer hotel was ideal. There was no plumbing, telephone or electricity, and the comforts of life in the house were exactly as "Reformation" John had left it. The water for washing and cleaning was collected "from a complicated system of gutters (some wooden and grooved by hand) from the intricate levels of the Adams house roof." Then it was dipped from a cistern for use. A spring provided drinking and cooking water. For the kitchen, the Captain made many of the utensils, including mustard spreaders. "Anything made of wood," Philip Johnson, a close friend, recalled, "he would carve it." When asked about the lack of modern facilities in this anachronistic House of Adams, the Captain always responded "I hate the inconveniences of conveniences." He wanted no part of frozen pipes and stopped-up sinks. Failure to provide modern services for his guests, especially women, brought criticism in Durham, but the Captain was unconcerned.[13]

"It was a mecca for people from all over the country," one guest recalled, "and those people had such a feeling for the Adamses that most of them corresponded with the family until their dying days." The boarders enjoyed parties and excursions, bathing in Great Bay, boat trips and vegetables from the Captain's garden. The "Lover's Walk," for those who qualified and sought it, circles the top of the cliffs over Great Bay. On Sunday afternoons a minister would preach at the Grove, a beautiful stand of pines on the Little Bay side of Adams Point. Guests and many outsiders attended worship at this inspirational spot. For his own part, Captain Adams sought peace elsewhere. "I've got to get away from the summer guests," he once confided to a friend. "They are a pain in the neck." He would set off in his "baby gundalow" sailboat for some fishing in the Bay. His cat, "Newmarket," named after the village where the stray was picked up, accompanied his master down to the shore and jumped into the water as Adams boarded his skiff.[14]

His son, Edward Cass Adams, known to all as "Cass," was a large chip off the Adams block. A massive, powerfully built man, Cass never left home. He became his father's partner in business affairs at the Point. A second generation boatbuilder, he left Adams Point only for his education. After attending Durham Point School House, he went to Dover High School. During this period of his life, he and his mother moved to Durham to live in the General John Sullivan House so the boy could commute to school. On weekends, they returned to Adams Point. There Cass remained for the rest of his life. Interested in preserving the Bay and learning its history, Cass was a charter member of the Oyster River Fish and Game Club and a president of the Piscataqua Pioneers. As one of the hosts for the family hotel, Cass once confided to a friend, "My gosh, you never could tell what those boarders were going to do next. One summer they'd be riding horses all over the neighbors' farms, and the next they'd be rowing to Newmarket and back every day, and if a fog came on you'd have to go out and hunt for 'em."[15]

The Skipper sailing his "baby gundalow" off Adams Point. UNHMS.

The Adams hotel business closed after the 1917 season. With the death of Joseph Martin Reuter Adams, the hotel's founder, the Captain gave up this livelihood except for renting out a guest cottage near Shooting Point. Now 57, Edward Adams decided to devote his energies to farming, logging, and maintaining his property. But the tradition of hospitality remained unbroken. Visitors, invited or not, thronged to the Point, especially on weekends. The Captain and his family were gracious and entertained everybody.

The Captain's diary for 1930, written when he was seventy years old, has also survived. With the exception of gundalowing the *Fanny M.*, he maintained the same schedule he had followed as a young man. Entries include: "shined Modle of schooner"; he worked in the woods, cut logs, dug clams, picked up oysters, repaired "dores," fixed fences and repaired his guest cottage. His only divergence from this fixed routine occurred upon the arrival of a snowstorm, when he would "sleep

and eat." With winter snow blocking the dirt road out to civilization
from January to April, Cass would snowshoe into Durham once a week
for staples.[16]

This diary mentions some important friends of the Captain during his later years. About 1919, David McIntosh, the founder of McIntosh College in Dover, purchased Footmans Island in Great Bay for a
duck-hunting preserve. Accompanying McIntosh to the island were his
two sons, David, Jr., nicknamed "Bud," and Edward, known as "Ned."
Soon the McIntoshes made the acquaintance of the Captain and Cass,
their closest neighbors, living only a short distance across the water.
The families visited back and forth, drawn together by their mutual
interest in boats, fishing, and Great Bay. On 9 June 1930 the Captain
jotted down, "Some rain. Cass & I went to Dover to see Bud about
working on schoner." On June 26, "We hauled logs to raft[.] Bud helpt[.]
Cass & Bud went to Dover at night."[17]

A year later, in 1931, Captain Adams decided to build a scaled-
down gundalow as a pleasure boat. He named it the *Driftwood*. Now
over seventy, he could not tolerate the defeat implied by "retirement."
Cass and Bud were enlisted in the Captain's last great dream and project, his nautical monument to his old days on the river. Adams, never
one to waste an opportunity, remembered some bent trees where he had
selected and cut the timbers for the *Fanny M.*, half a century before. He
and his crew went back to this place and put up for the night at the
same house. As he had predicted, some of the old trees were still there,
ideal for knees and bow pieces. "Actually," Bud once remarked, "I didn't
do too much building. Mostly I just went into the woods with Adams
while he looked for trees." Bud tended to deprecate his talents. "My
father presented me with an axe at age six," McIntosh said. "I have never
become an expert axe man, because I got such a late start!" After
attending Harvard and Dartmouth, Bud returned to Dover Point for his
true calling, becoming a highly sought-after boatbuilder.[18]

During the 1930s, while the *Driftwood* was under construction,
changes occurred in the Adams household. In 1931 Olive Esther Libbey
Adams, the Captain's mother, died at 90. After her death, Adams would
often say with a twinkle in his eye that he was left an orphan at seventy.
A few years later, Adams was saddened with the passing of his wife,
Frances. They had been married more than fifty years. Suffering a
shock during November 1934, she died on 11 May 1935. A great lover of
poetry and books, she had taught in various schools. During its last
years of operation, she was a great hostess for the summer hotel and

Driftwood under construction during the 1930s. Bow and stern logs shaped and held in place by shores, with planking of the sides carried up nearly to deck level. Arnold L. Belcher photo. UNHMS.

was known as a "royal entertainer." It was a lonely household for some time. Then, on 9 August 1936 Cass married Analesa Marie Foss. Originally from Foss Beach in Rye, Analesa was a 1921 graduate of Boston University. She was a successful businesswoman and had worked in Boston as a statistician before her marriage. She and Cass had been long-time friends since their families had often visited back and forth. As active as the Adamses, Analesa was a member of the Durham Historical Society, the Piscataqua Pioneers, and the Newfields chapter of the DAR. After her arrival the Adams home was again enlivened with hospitality.[19]

In addition to the usual visitors, several nautical enthusiasts appeared at Adams Point during the 1930s. Their purpose was to interview Captain Adams in an effort to preserve knowledge of the gundalow before it was lost to history. In 1936 the Massachusetts branch of the Historic American Merchant Marine Survey, Works Progress Administration, recognized this need. This organization, under the sponsorship of the Smithsonian Institution, authorized the first scientific study of the Piscataqua River gundalow. During July of that year, D. Foster Taylor, baffled at every turn in gathering material, was finally directed to Adams Point. Taylor spent the latter part of the month conversing with Adams, collecting data, and measuring and photographing the *Driftwood*.

In 1935, William G. Saltonstall, a member of the History
Department of the Phillips Exeter Academy, "took Capt. Adams for a
sail on Great Bay in my catboat. What a man!" Their friendship aided
Saltonstall in researching and writing his book, *Ports of Piscataqua*
(1941). From the late 1920s onward Clyde Whitehouse, a Dover optome-
trist and owner of a schooner power boat, frequently motored down to
the Point to see the Captain. Whitehouse salvaged some old boards from
the derelict *Fanny M.* and constructed a model of the last gundalow
from her original timbers. The Whitehouse family climbed up on the
staging to observe the latest work on the *Driftwood*. Adams revelled in
these visits.[20]

Although Adams had no interest in writing his autobiography,
he wanted the record of the past preserved. The loss of recent history
disturbed him. "We were concentrating on the distant past," he said.
"Historians were doing research on the seventeenth century, while the
last hundred years were being ignored. Soon there would be no record
of its contribution to progress." Again on this subject, he commented,
"We know about the Revolutionary War, but no one has written about
the generation of my parents."[21]

The rapid passing of his own era concerned him in 1933. On April
22 he wrote to the Bureau of Navigation and Steamboat Inspection,
Department of Commerce, Washington, to protest "against the erection
of a fixed bridge over the Piscataqua River at Dover Point." For any tall
ship wanting to enter Great Bay, the erection of the proposed General
John Sullivan Bridge would represent a final blow. The Washington
bureaucracy responded by referring his letter to the U.S. Engineers of
the War Department, which had jurisdiction for these matters. On May
8 Adams attended a hearing in Portsmouth on the bridge controversy in
vain. The next year the bridge was built.[22]

The Captain's special world was threatened a decade later. In
1946 advocates prepared to press for approval their Great Bay development plan by the 1947 State Legislature. According to their proposal,
the state would build dams to end pollution and to check erosion. Such a
massive state project, its proponents insisted, would revitalize the once
great fishing industry and promote tourism, providing a summer play-
ground for the 400,000 residents of New Hampshire.

The reaction of the Adamses to the so-called "Great Bay Plan"
was both instantaneous and predictable. They led the movement to
oppose it. Reaction from the 800 shoreline property owners brought
cries of "treason," "a racket," and "Just socialism or fascism or whatever

you want to call it." Almost overnight "No Trespassing" signs sprang up to warn outsiders.[23]

A reporter sought out Captain Adams and Cass, and spoke with them at their Adams Point home. Impressed by the old homestead, he noticed a seven-foot long flintlock musket, "declared to be one of three known to be in existence," adorning a wall in the hallway. The Adamses inherited the independence of this Revolutionary War ancestor who had carried this piece at Bunker Hill.

"The problem here is pollution and that is all there is to it," they replied to the reporter's question. The Adamses objected to the pollution of their property caused by the cities of Exeter, Dover and Portsmouth and outside the Great Bay shoreline property owners' jurisdiction. The plan was detrimental to the Adams' interests.

"They were going to take charge of everything," Cass explained, "even personal property." When asked if this project would not attract tourism, Cass said, "We are not interested in the tourist business. Construction of a dam would cause the waters to freeze and there would be no real tidewaters. The proposed dam at Dover Point would result in a cesspool without an outlet. Some feared it might cause high water."[24]

If the Great Bay Plan had succeeded, the Adamses would have found themselves on a landlocked lake, with all river traffic to Portsmouth ended unless a lock system were installed at the proposed Dover Point Dam. However, the state did no more with this grandiose plan than to publish it. The Great Bay Plan went the way of the ill-starred Franklin City.

After this crisis, father and son continued work on the *Driftwood* through the rest of the decade. Cass set aside any plans he might have had to adhere to his father's ambition to complete the boat.

During June 1948, Captain Adams, now 87 years old, "took a fancy to sail down the bay" to visit William Watson, the son of the late Harrison Watson, a gundalowman. "I won't live forever," the Skipper said when Cass objected to the trip. The old man handled his "baby gundalow" well and completed the six-mile trip in about half an hour without incident. Unaware of this last nostalgic voyage, the Captain's friends spotted him three miles up the bay. Upon Adams's arrival, the Watsons insisted that their unexpected guest remain for a traditional New England supper, "a big pot of all-day cooked beans, steaming brown bread, freshly fried doughnuts and coffee." The Captain ate the meal with relish, claiming that such food was the secret of his longevity. Completely in character, Adams "saw nothing unusual in his trip and considered the reports an invasion of his privacy."[25]

Captain Adams at work on one of the ship models which he built as a hobby.
Douglas Armsden photo. DAC.

The launching of the *Driftwood* in the fall of 1950 on his ninetieth birthday, amidst great fanfare, was a great day in his life. His dream was now fulfilled. After that his health went steadily downhill.

In early spring, he was taken to a rest home in Newmarket, suffering from pneumonia and heart disease. At his side to the end was the faithful Cass. Just before he died Captain Adams told Cass, who was ill with a bad cold, to go home, "or you won't be able to attend my funeral." On 9 April 1951 at five in the afternoon, Edward Hamlin Adams died. With the coming of night the spirit of the last and most famous gundalow captain drifted over the waters of Great Bay to join the rivermen of his youth.[26]

The Fanny M., *the last working gundalow*

The building of the gundalow, *Fanny M.*, has assured Captain Adams's niche in Piscataqua nautical history. Construction of this vessel began at Adams Point during the spring of 1883. According to legend, Adams "built her almost single-handed, except to the assistance of an elderly man, the only experienced shipwright available." One day the hired man asked for a day off to pick apples. He fell from a tree and did not return to his job the next day. He had broken his neck. Adams completed the work alone. So much for what Adams asserted were the facts. Bud McIntosh, who has lifted his share of heavy timbers for over half a century at his boatyard, disputes this version. "Lifting the knees," Bud says, "and setting everything into place would have been too much for one man."[27]

Too innovative to build a standard gundalow, Adams added improvements as he went along. When he finished his vessel in 1886, the *Fanny M.* was undoubtedly the most modern gundalow on the river. With a carrying capacity of sixty tons, the vessel was 69 feet 10 inches in length, 19 feet across the beam, and 4 feet 5 inches from the deck to the hull. Constructing the gundalow before the age of power tools, the Captain spent hundreds, perhaps thousands of hours, in hand work.

Adams often told a favorite story regarding the corner plugs. One afternoon Adams positioned the *Fanny M.* over a mud flat to drain her bilges. With him on board were his two hired hands. When the water cleared, the most reliable man was to redrive the plugs and turn in for a night's sleep. Hours later, Adams awoke in his cabin bunk in the pitch dark cuddy. He knew something was wrong since the *Fanny M.* had a "solid dead feeling." There was no sound except for the heavy breathing and snoring of his two men asleep in their spring beds in the cabin. Dropping a line into the cabin, Adams noticed it was wet upon retrieval. Upon raising the lantern, the Captain discerned the forms of the two sleeping men in their beds with water up to the mattresses. An ordinary captain would have exploded with wrath, but Adams bided his time. The rising water covered the mattresses, and soon flowed into an open mouth. A loud commotion followed. In their fright, the two men slid off their mattresses and into the deeper water. Neglect to perform an easy routine chore had not only cost them a night's sleep, but also taught them a near-fatal lesson they would never forget.[28]

The leeboard of the *Fanny M.*, made of 3-inch oak, was 5 feet wide and about 16½ feet long. If the board were to warp Adams knew a

Model of the **Fanny M.** *at Portsmouth Athenaeum. The large photo shows the entire model, followed clockwise by gundalowman at stern; the interior of the cuddy with built-in bunks and living quarters; bow with cutwater, stump mast and yard with furled sail; leeboard with iron bands and braces; and cargo space below deck next to cuddy. L. Franklin Heald photos. PA.*

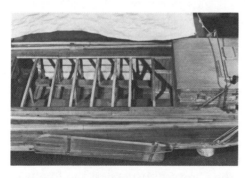

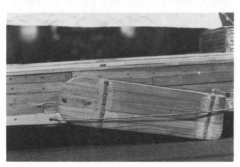

foolproof method to correct it. Once a leeboard had been damaged, Adams recalled, by striking a submerged rock. The board was removed for repair, but no way could be found to straighten it. After sundry trial-and-error methods had failed, the captain decided "to lay it on a hard flat spot in the river and allow the loaded gundalow to settle upon it at low tide." The damage was thus repaired, and thereafter this method was used by all rivermen for straightening bent leeboards.[29]

A special feature of the *Fanny M.* consisted of the excellent living accommodations in the cuddy. Unlike most other captains who neglected comfort, Adams took pride in providing the best for himself and his crew. His cabin contained four bunks, with lockers for personal gear. The interior was painted and the floor covered with linoleum. A cherrywood dining table, mirrors and a wash basin added to the amenities. A standard of cleanliness was maintained.

Most gundalows had a ladder or companionway leading from the deck to the floor of the cuddy, but this usual feature was not sufficient for Adams. He built, perhaps invented, a vertical stairway, with alternate steps as one ascended or descended. This up and down stairway provided a triangle step and relative safety for slippery boots.[30]

Still another improvement Captain Adams devised for the *Fanny M.* was the location of the smoke pipe of the galley stove. The stove, which served for both heating and cooking, was fitted to a chimney which passed through the cuddy roof. Most builders of gundalows did not plan ahead, so many a chimney emerged outside and brushed against one of the iron blocks in the sail rigging. This caused no end of trouble, resulting in many collisions and usually filling the interior of the cuddy with smoke and soot. Often a half-suffocated crew would be compelled to flee to the deck for relief. To correct this common mistake, Adams located the stove nearly amidships. The smoke pipe came up through a hatch, and drew well, When the hatch cover was removed the interior of the cabin received more light. In addition, the open hatch allowed the cooking fumes to escape. The ventilation of the *Fanny M.* was a marked improvement over that of other gundalows.[31]

To insure a supply of fresh water, the *Fanny M.* carried four small water casks. An iron bilge pump was also part of its standard equipment.

The *Fanny M.* was unique in another respect. She was the only gundalow to carry a gasoline engine for propulsion. For all practical purposes, the internal combustion engine came into use too late to be adopted by gundalows. Since the *Fanny M.* was still on the river in the

Derelict Fanny M. *at Dover Point in the 1920s listing heavily starboard, prior to her breaking up in the ice a few years later. Note that much equipment and many boards already had been stripped from her hull. Anon. collection.*

1900s, Adams was able to take advantage of this improvement. In her last days, Adams "installed a converted automobile engine, though the sails were not removed."[32]

But the *Fanny M.* enjoys a far greater distinction than being the last working gundalow because the boat has provided vital information to historians and maritime scholars trying to preserve knowledge of this special type of river transportation. In the mid-1920s (the date is probably 1925), Professors Gordon Wilkes, who summered at Newington across the bay, and A. V. de Forest of the Massachusetts Institute of Technology traveled to Dover Point to examine the wreck of the *Fanny M.* Wilkes made extensive measurements of her hull. Both he and de Forest photographed the vessel from every angle. During 1934–1935 Wilkes built a scale model of the *Fanny M.* Many years later this model was donated to the Portsmouth Athenaeum.

In 1936 D. Foster Taylor visited Adams Point for his W.P.A. report. The Captain entrusted his 1882 gundalow model (made preparatory to the building of the *Fanny M.*) and a river packet model to Taylor for presentation to the Smithsonian Institution. These authentic models, painstakingly made by Adams are thus preserved for all time as part of the Watercraft Collection there, and are available for inspection by the public. This collection is perhaps the finest in the world, and the Captain's donation of his models insures further study and interest in the gundalow.[33]

With this vast amount of information at his disposal — the measurements, photographs, models and interviews with Adams — Taylor commissioned the drafting of two large blueprints of the *Fanny M.* Completed in 1937, one shows the lines, body plan and outboard profile of this craft, while the other is a sail plan. Depositing the original prints with the Smithsonian, Taylor published the drawings in reduced size in his 1942 article. Thus the lines of the *Fanny M.* are documented, and these plans were used in the building of the gundalow replica more than forty years later. Without such plans authentic reconstruction would have been immeasureably more difficult.

The Building of the Driftwood

In 1931 the seventy-year-old captain began the twenty-year construction of a pleasure gundalow, the *Driftwood*. With the help of Cass, and a neighbor, Harry Mathas (who soon dropped out), Adams planned to complete his boat within a few years. But construction dragged on. After a hiatus of ten years, the Adamses resumed the job and finally launched the *Driftwood* in 1950.

Captain Adams incorporated some new ideas in his design of the *Driftwood*. The original planned dimensions of the gundalow were "43 feet 2 inches, length overall; 14 feet at the great beam; and depth, from one deck to top of keel, 5 feet 9 inches." Although gundalows had no keels in their history, Adams made a departure from previous practice for this vessel. He also decided to build a bowsprit for the *Driftwood*, a radical departure from type. Finally he made provisions for two propellers in the hull, since the craft would be powered by two gasoline engines. To retain the appearance of a gundalow, however, he intended to give her a schooner rig, equipped with sails. The Captain and Cass expected to take out "parties of sightseers for cruises on the river during the summer season, and carry whatever freight is offered."[35]

The initial schedule for completion during the first few years seemed plausible. In 1936, a reporter on the scene indicated the launch-

(Above) Interior of the Driftwood looking aft, with Captain Adams at right. (Left) Rough-hewn bow logs of the Driftwood. Arnold L. Belcher photos. UNHMS.

ing was scheduled for August. But as time went by, the Adamses were devoting only odd moments to the job. Much time had been spent in securing the bent timbers.

After this saga had gone on for nineteen years, Great Bay neighbors and reporters wanted to pin the Captain down for a launching date. They couldn't. To references about his age, Adams replied, "If I wasn't getting older every day, I'd be dead." Observers noticed he was still spry, but a little stooped, "possibly from working in the confined quarters of a gundalow." He was able to go up a ladder faster than most kids.[36]

The truth of the matter was that during the last few years, the Captain and Cass were only occasionally working on the boat. Evelyn Browne, a neighbor, often stopped by the Adams home, and the Captain and Cass were usually "swapping stories as they sat around on the ground, or in the woodshed." During winters, of course, all work stopped, and the Captain spent his time woodcarving. He cut out almost enough ducks, eagles, and fish to fill two rooms of the house. The little space left was taken by ship models — coasting schooners, gundalows, and other vessels—which used to ply the ports of Great Bay. His models were built during two periods of his life, his youth and old age. "In between those years, I was too busy making a living to have any time for models," Adams said. "It was a great inconvenience making a living."[37]

In retrospect, it seems as if the wily Captain deliberately delayed the last minute details of its completion to save the launch for a special occasion. He wanted to launch the *Driftwood* on 22 October 1950, his ninetieth birthday. The final dimensions of the craft were a bit different than originally planned twenty years before. The green and white boat measured 43 feet, 9 inches long; 13 feet, 10 inches wide, and 5 feet deep. It weighed twelve tons. Shorter than the *Fanny M.*, the *Driftwood* was also higher "to allow cabin space below decks." There Adams had constructed six built-in bunks. The plans for a bowsprit and sail rigging were abandoned. A Gray engine and a Model A Ford engine provided power. Cass worked on the interior of the boat the day before the launching, getting the cabin ready. Visitors came down the cabin stairs to look around, as Cass struggled to complete his inside work. He was exhausted at day's end. Everything was ready.[38]

Sunday, 22 October 1950 saw Adams Point explode with people— friends, well-wishers, newspapermen, and just plain admirers—arriving by land and water. The shores and hillside below the house were swarming with people. Cars were parked back in the fields, row after

Cass Adams, left, and Captain Adams, center, on one of their many breaks during the twenty-year construction of the Driftwood. *UNHMS.*

Captain Adams with an adz, hand-hewing a knee of the Driftwood. *UNHMS.*

Interior view of the Driftwood's *stern, transom, and rudderpost. UNHMS.*

Cass Adams caulking the bottom seams of the Driftwood *in 1950. DAC.*

Adams Point on 22 October 1950, at the launching of the Driftwood, *with a gathering of 2000 well-wishers by land and by water to observe the event. Douglas Armsden photos. DAC.*

row. Off the Point, a flotilla of sailboats, private yachts, the Portsmouth Navigation Company vessel, and the Isles of Shoals excursion boat were waiting. Estimates of the number of people there on that day range from one to two thousand.

At the house, commotion reigned supreme. Analesa Adams was busy all day, making red flannel hash for the launching crew, headed by Bud and Ned McIntosh. The friends of the Captain presented him with a "money tree," with ninety new one-dollar bills. Another gift was a ship model, "floating" on a sea of money. Some sixty birthday cakes were produced in the Adams' kitchen, along with coffee for 500 people, but more visitors kept arriving than expected. The celebrants brought more than forty cakes themselves. (According to one story, months after the celebration was over, someone supposedly went into one of the many rooms of the mansion and found twenty-five cakes, put away for the time being and forgotten.)

The crowd then assembled at the launching site where the *Driftwood* was bedecked with flags. An Adams family pennant flew from the bow. Cass Adams was the informal master of ceremonies. Standing on the bow deck, he told the audience, "I would like to have the gundalow go down as a symbol of the freedom of those days." Loud applause greeted his observation, "All men here are equal, and all titles were left at the gate." This statement referred to two dignitaries, Dr. Arthur S. Adams (no close relation to the Captain), President of the University of New Hampshire, and Representative Chester Merrow of the First Congressional District, who spoke briefly on this occasion. After various presentations and a singing of "Happy Birthday," everyone looked to Captain Adams. "All I can say is, thank you," he remarked.[39]

It was now 10:30 A.M., the high tide of the day. Lois Kent, a twenty-two year old Plymouth State Teachers College student, whose family had been neighbors of the Adams clan for five generations, christened the vessel with a bottle of champagne (some say it was really hard cider) with a smash across the prow. With Cass, the McIntoshes, and others aboard, the *Driftwood* slid down the greased skid to the cheers of the crowd. A *National Geographic* photographer recorded the scene. The air was filled as well with the tooting of boat whistles and car horns. When it slid into the water, the *Driftwood* was the first gundalow on Great Bay in about thirty-five years. Even young children jumping up and down sensed the historic moment.[40]

The *Driftwood* went into the water smoothly, her engines started on schedule, and all went perfectly—for the first half hour. In her tour of

The christening of the Driftwood *by sponsor Lois Kent at Adams Cove. A stooped Captain Edward H. Adams, wearing sailor hat, beside her, with Cass Adams above on bow deck. Douglas Armsden photo. DAC.*

the cove, the engines began to burn up. Someone had forgotten to turn on the seacocks, or valves to the engines' cooling system intake, and they overheated. The gundalow limped back to shore. Her maiden voyage turned out to be her last. The crowd went up to the big house for refreshments. The old Captain asked for a piece of bread.

"How much did the gundalow cost?" a newsman asked Cass.

"Gosh, I don't know. Seems though it cost more than a government battleship!"[41]

The most exciting day at Adams Point in years was over. A few days later, the Captain received a letter from Governor Sherman Adams (also no close relation) of New Hampshire, regretting that he could not be present on that great day, but wishing the Captain "smooth sailing for both you and the Gundalow during the coming year." But the Governor's hope was in vain. Within a week after her launching, the *Driftwood* was hauled up on shore above the high tide mark and neglected. Later the boat was jacked up on blocks. Like yachts today, it started to rot from the top down. After Captain Adams died in the spring of 1951, Cass did not perform proper maintenance on the boat. When Thomas W. Dudley consulted Cass on a legal matter at the Point during the winter of 1953–1954, he inspected the *Driftwood*. Dudley recalled,

> The gundalow was not being cared for, and was in the worst possible place. It was rotting away, and I was very disturbed by it. I never saw such intricate and painstaking woodwork on a boat in my life, the craftsmanship involved, and the time it took to build something like that. Not just aluminum or plastic, or fiberglass as one sees today. Cass was unconcerned, and it didn't seem to bother him. He had other things on his mind.[42]

The Adams line was dying out with Cass, for he and Analesa had no children. Combining his interests in wildlife and hunting with his talent for art, Cass delighted in carving duck decoys and turtles. A painter in water colors and oils, he specialized in ships, especially gundalows. The John Hancock Warehouse Museum at York, Maine, originally owned by the revolutionary leader on the banks of the York River, commissioned Cass to build a model gundalow. Cass modeled it along the lines of the *Fanny M.* and crafted the hull over six feet long. With the hull nearing completion, Cass was taken ill. He died suddenly at the Exeter Hospital on 25 July 1959.[43]

Cass Adams was buried in the family tomb, with hundreds of people paying their last respects. In a very real sense, the rites for Cass, the last of the Adamses, symbolized as well the end of Adams Point. On that summer day, the mourners placed a huge bouquet of flowers on the forward deck of the *Driftwood*. The flag at the stern was lowered to half mast.

Analesa Adams, Cass's widow, had no desire to remain alone in an antiquated 21-room house. "The house," she said, "would have been quite an expense because it was a big house, and you can't have a house and not keep it up." She felt the same way about the *Driftwood*. To preserve it, she offered to sell the gundalow to the Mystic Seaport Museum of Mystic, Connecticut, for $10,000. The deal fell through. Later she hoped to donate the vessel to the Strawbery Banke museum in Portsmouth. The Banke was not interested.

Picturesque Adams Point with the homestead and the Driftwood *sitting on blocks at the water's edge, 1961, after the property had been acquired by the N.H. Fish and Game Department. Douglas Armsden photo. DAC.*

Concerning the Adams Point property, Analesa recalled, "The Audubon Society at the last minute wanted it, but we had already promised it to the state." In 1961, Analesa Adams sold the eighty acres to the New Hampshire Fish and Game Commission, but reserved the right to use the house as long as she lived. The next year she married Richard MacLeod, a United States customs official, and moved to her new home at Derby Line, Vermont, on the Canadian border, leaving the Adams House empty. Two years later in 1964, Avis Suzanne Adams, Cass's unmarried sister, died. The doors of the Adams tomb were opened for the last time for her interment. During her active years, Avis Suzanne was an art teacher at public schools in Massachusetts and Connecticut. Taken ill, she had been institutionalized for the last thirty years of her life in a mental sanatorium in Concord, New Hampshire.[44]

Left vacant, the Adams property was repeatedly vandalized. The Adams House became a place of wild parties as "doors and windows were smashed, furniture torn apart, [and] bricks pulled from the old fireplace." Private efforts to save and repair the house failed. Vandals also damaged the doors to the Adams tomb. The decision was made to bulldoze earth up against the entrance to seal it effectively. Remarked one Durham citizen, "We wouldn't want the old captain's skull being used for a football up at the university."[45]

In 1967, Analesa MacLeod gave her permission to the Fish and Game Commission for the demolition of the Adams mansion. Sometime during those years she also held an auction and sold the disposable items of the Adams house and estate: furniture, farm implements, and anything which brought a sale. Philip Johnson, a longtime neighbor, purchased many of the Captain's handmade wooden tools as well as the baby gundalow. As the craft was too decrepit to move in one piece, Johnson first took the lines from the boat and then salvaged the best timbers.

In the wake of these developments, in October 1967, the *Driftwood* was floated and hauled from Adams Point up the Oyster River to the historic Town Landing in Durham. Bud and Ned McIntosh conducted the two-hour move with power boats along either side of the *Driftwood*. "She was already badly rotted," Ned McIntosh said, "but buoyant enough to float." In Durham a concerned group wanted to save the vessel. Controversy, however, broke out immediately on where the gundalow should be cradled. Some area residents at the Landing objected to having the *Driftwood* "in their front yard," deeming it a safety hazard to children, and petitioned successfully to have it moved. After about a month at the Landing, the gundalow no one seemed to want was hauled to Jackson's Landing, the relatively isolated town recreational park located about a mile downstream on the Oyster River.

On Monday, 11 November 1968 at 2:00 A.M., the Durham Fire Department was called out by a local resident. The gundalow was on fire, in a great ball of roaring flame. By the time the firemen reached the scene the deck had fallen in. At daybreak, they wet down the smouldering timbers. A charred and broken frame was all that remained; the devastation was so complete that restoration was impossible. Investigators noted the origin of the fire was of a "suspicious nature," since the blaze occurred during a period of "an extremely wet spell of weather." Clearly it was arson. Whoever poured the gasoline and set the torch to the gundalow was never apprehended for this senseless crime. The *Driftwood* had joined her builders.[46]

The rotted hull of the Driftwood *on the shore at Adams Point, October 1967, shortly before her last voyage to Durham. Peter E. Randall photo.*

Analesa Adams MacLeod never returned, and widowed again, died in Exeter on 6 July 1981. She was buried in Vermont.

During the spring of 1968, workmen tore down the Adams mansion and leveled the site for a parking lot. With the past bulldozed away, the University of New Hampshire began construction that same year of the Jackson Estuarine Laboratory. The *Jere A. Chase*, a vessel operated by the University for its research, is docked during the summer near the site of the old gundalow anchorage. Overhead the gulls soar and squawk as if nothing had ever happened.[47]

Evaluation of Captain Adams and his Gundalows

"We never knew who was coming," Analesa Adams, the Captain's daughter-in-law, once remarked. "We just seemed to be open house." Captain Adams was the host to the whole world at his Great Bay home, whether his visitors were other gundalowmen, hunters, fishermen, summer boarders, nautical scholars, or shipbuilders. Once even a group of Indians from Old Town, Maine, canoed to the grove, camped there, and headed for Exeter to board a train for Washington in order to present a bill. The Captain met and knew them all.[48]

Adams was a man born to the nineteenth century who never in his thinking and actions really entered the twentieth century. "Make do," a New England adage, symbolized his life and reflected his conservative viewpoint.

More than any other captain, Edward Hamlin Adams helped to generate the present-day interest in gundalows. Mythologized by the press as a folk hero of the river, he left the people of the Piscataqua region a sense of curiosity about its maritime past. It is no wonder that the replica of this historically important craft is named the *Captain Edward H. Adams*.

Captain Edward H. Adams, *gundalow replica, under sail for the first time during her Durham-Portsmouth run in July 1982. Douglas Armsden photo. DAC.*

III *The Building and Launching of the Captain Edward H. Adams*

A Project is Born

THE BUILDING OF A GUNDALOW REPLICA, *Captain Edward H. Adams*, from the original idea to the completed vessel, extended over six years and cost $100,000. Coordinating work on this boat with an educational support program required much effort. The story of the Piscataqua Gundalow Project is a modern-day saga of spiraling costs, scarcity of materials and revival of half-forgotten techniques. Despite these obstacles, the Piscataqua community rallied to the *Adams* and completed the boat in 1982.

In 1976 Dr. Albert E. Hickey wrestled with a housing problem. His home was the restored 112-foot barge *Rising Castle*, a Hudson River boat built in 1924 by the Lehigh Valley Railroad. For some time the *Rising Castle* had been moored at the Champernowne Pier at Eliot, Maine, on the Piscataqua. When he learned that the owner of the pier would no longer lease moorage for his houseboat, Hickey was forced to look elsewhere. Hickey drove to Newmarket to see his friend, Richard Gallant, a Newmarket businessman and an ardent sailor. Gallant welcomed Hickey but soon realized that the *Rising Castle* was too large to moor off his riverfront property on the Lamprey. "We talked about his barge, and this and that for an hour," Gallant said. "We talked about the old days and the gundalows, their shape and design, and how nice it would be to build a replica of one."[1]

Hickey eventually found a berth at the Prescott Park landing in Portsmouth, but the conversation lingered in his mind. A consultant and publisher of educational books, Hickey had some experience of preserving historic relics and planning replicas. He had purchased and

117

restored the 33-ton dory Banks schooner *Tamarack*, the last vessel built in Newfoundland to fish under sail. Another preservation project included the Bangor and Aroostook Railroad Caboose Car No. 34, built in 1914, which became part of the Conway Scenic Railroad at North Conway, New Hampshire. His life aboard the *Rising Castle* , which he purchased in 1971, aroused his interest in gundalows and his awareness of their important role in times past.[2]

Hickey realized that the city of Portsmouth was the logical place to sell the idea of a new project. His office was located in the Ward-Whidden House on "The Hill," a collection of restored colonial and early American houses near the downtown business district. Anxious to preserve its architectural heritage, Portsmouth supported the development of Strawbery Banke, a complex of old buildings. Since its inception in 1958, Strawbery Banke had evolved into a major tourist and educational attraction for the city, drawing 70,000 visitors annually. What Strawbery Banke needed to complement its restored houses and craft demonstrations, Hickey thought, was a gundalow to illustrate New Hampshire's maritime heritage. In 1975, Paul Dunn, a friend of Hickey's, had organized an exhibit called "The Boston Tea Party Ship." The exhibit consists of a ninety-foot replica of the brig *Beaver*, one of the original Tea Party ships, and a barge museum in Boston. Visitors come from all over the globe to view *Beaver II*, making it a commercial success. Heartened by the popular appeal of his friend's project during the fall of 1977, Hickey visited the Dr. John Jackson House which then housed the administrative offices of Strawbery Banke. "I went to see Peggy Armitage in the beginning," Hickey said. "She was very good as an organizer, a people's person."[3]

Hickey had chosen well. As Ms. Armitage recalled:

> Al Hickey came to see me when I was the Director of Strawbery Banke. The reaction of the other people in the Banke was: 'How reliable and safe a risk is a person who lives on a barge?' But I bought the plan. It looked viable, educational, and worthwhile, and I convinced the Board of Trustees to accept it. They did, on condition that one of the Strawbery Banke trustees was appointed a member of the Working Committee of the Piscataqua Gundalow Project. Other people had come forward with similar ideas, but Al was the one who succeeded in having it accepted by the Banke. And the rest is history.[4]

The Support of the University of New Hampshire

The next step of Al Hickey and Peggy Armitage was to secure funding for the project. The nearest and most logical source for aid was the University of New Hampshire. "Al Hickey came in," Dr. Robert Corell said, "walked in off the street and indicated his interest in building a replica of a gundalow and his commitment to it." A professor of Mechanical Engineering at the University since 1966, Corell directs the Marine Program, which includes the Jackson Estuarine Laboratory and the Shoals Marine Laboratory at the Isles of Shoals. Corell is familiar with the role that gundalows have played in New Hampshire's past.[5]

"We filled out the papers three days before they were due," Hickey said. He and Corell applied for a $1000 grant from the Spaulding-Potter Charitable Trust which "granted . . . a sum of money to enable the university . . . to improve the economic, cultural and community life of the State of New Hampshire." On 29 October 1977 Corell jotted a memo to accompany the papers for the "*Driftwood* Gundalow Project," barely meeting the November 1st deadline.[6]

Once the grant was approved, Corell sought other support for the project. On 16 November he announced the project to people both inside and outside the university community, including professors, historians, boatbuilders and state officials. "We will do what we can to support the development of this idea, the concept of which I find very interesting and exciting," Corell wrote. "It is conceivable that something might grow out of this project and blend in with our ongoing marine education efforts."[7]

"The *Driftwood* Gundalow," as the project was first known, printed a prospectus. The Kittery Historical and Naval Museum at Kittery, Maine, through its president, John F. Hallett, joined forces with UNH and Strawbery Banke. The original Board of Overseers evolved into a Board of Directors in early 1978, with Corell as its Director and Hickey as its Program Coordinator. "Al telephoned me," Dick Gallant said. "He said he had seen Bob Corell at UNH, and was getting a project organized. He asked me to join him." Corell, Gallant, Hickey, attorney Thomas W. Dudley and Strawbery Banke trustee Cyrus Sweet of New Castle constituted the original Board of Directors, assisted by a Working Committee and an Advisory Council. Dr. Lewis Roberts, Jr., director of the Thompson School at the University, also joined the project in its early stages. The old name of the *Driftwood* was struck from grant applications and press releases, as this title was an ominous reminder of the blaze and failure a decade previously. The Piscataqua Gundalow Project, as it was now officially known, named the proposed replica the *Captain Edward H. Adams* to honor the late skipper.[8]

From the outset, the Directors sought the advice of David "Bud" McIntosh, a veteran who had built more than eighty wooden boats during fifty years at his Dover Point yard. McIntosh said he was chosen to oversee the building phase of the project because of his association with Captain Adams. "I guess I'm supposed to know how to build one," McIntosh laconically explained. "At least no one else claims it." Others are less reticent in their descriptions of Bud's ability. "When it comes to boats," said a local marine expert, "Bud McIntosh is it."[9]

McIntosh estimated that the construction could be completed in two years. Strawbery Banke, more accessible than Adams Point, was selected for the construction site. The Project directors contacted the Smithsonian Institution and obtained Taylor's 1937 measured drawings of the *Fanny M.* The construction budget for the whole boat was estimated at $50,000 over a two-year period; in 1978 $25,000 was allocated to provide $7,000 for lumber and $18,000 for labor costs. But building the gundalow was only part of the overall plan; Corell also wanted the gundalow to serve an educational function. To this end, the University of New Hampshire reached into the surrounding communities by means of marine docents (college or university-sponsored teachers and lecturers who speak before outside groups). Seventy docents, all volunteers, have been appearing before school classes, civic organizations, clubs, church groups, and virtually any other audience throughout New Hampshire and Maine which expresses interest. With exhibits and slide presentations the docents have promoted the Piscataqua Gundalow Project and other marine-related topics. Dr. Joseph A. Del Porto and Kennard Palfrey have given their gundalow presentation more than sixty times.[10]

From the start, the educational mission of the project was paramount. Dr. Charles E. Clark, a member of the Educational Advisory Council and Chairman of the UNH History Department, explained,

> the gundalow itself ought to be the focus of the educational program. If it is not, then the construction project and all the fanfare about it, which is at the center of the enterprise at the moment, will become for intellectual purposes only a side issue.[11]

Once the *Adams* was launched, the unique value of the gundalow replica as part of the outreach program of marine education would be realized. The *Adams* could be sailed to locations in the communities on the estuary. Visiting these towns once every two years in the spring or fall, accompanied by a shore-based exhibit, the gundalow would attract attention. As Corell and Hickey knew, several precedents indicated the gundalow project would succeed. The previously mentioned *Beaver II*, the Boston Tea Party ship replica, had been a financial success. Perhaps more to the point was the Hudson River sloop replica, *Clearwater*, built in the early 1970s for Pete Seeger, the folksinger and conservationist. Seeger sailed into ports along the 150-mile stretch of the Hudson from New York City to Albany and presented shows and concerts with fiddlers, ballad singers, and blues guitar pickers to schoolchildren, sailing buffs, and townspeople. "We figure that if the Hudson is going to be saved from being a permanent sewer," Seeger wrote, "people must learn to love it again, to come down to the water's edge and see it close." Seeger later became a member of the Education Advisory Council for the *Adams*.[12]

The organizers of the Piscataqua Gundalow Project believe that the docent educational program should be involved not only with Piscataqua history and past technology, but also with current public issues of industrial waste, water supply, and food resources. "Those who live in the Bay area today," Thomas W. Dudley said, "don't realize or appreciate how important the bays and the rivers once were as waterways and for transportation. Now they're just something to dump pollutants in." Al Hickey voiced a similar opinion: "Most people—or many people—don't realize that one can travel to Durham or Exeter by water as they did long ago. Nowadays they just want the highway route number to make the trip to Dover."[13]

One early objective of the Project was to resolve its legal status. Serving as Clerk for the organization, Thomas W. Dudley traveled to Concord to clarify the Project's purpose. "I did the legal work," Dudley said, "and shepherded it through. The project is set up as a non-profit organization, and is able to accept financial donations on a tax-exempt basis."[14]

In addition to its fund-raising activities, the Project officers presented programs and maintained close ties with town officials. In terms of generating public interest for the Project, these efforts were successful.[15] On 3 November 1978 William A. Baker spoke at the Kittery Historical and Naval Museum on "Gundalows and Other Working Craft" to a capacity audience of 350 people. A member of the Education Advisory Council, Baker was a noted naval architect and marine historian. Associated with the Massachusetts Institute of Technology, Baker

Early construction stage of the Captain Adams *in the Strawbery Banke Boat-yard, showing bottom planking and floor with cross timbers. UNHD.*

had designed the *Mayflower II* and supervised its construction in England. Now his vast knowledge was eagerly sought as developments proceeded toward the building of the *Adams*.[16]

Chips Fly Outside the Strawbery Banke Yard

A fine crash in the deep woods sounded the first note of the gundalow replica. Nathaniel K. Brown donated the trees from his woodlot for this purpose. Lewis Roberts and Martin Curran of the UNH School of Forestry had found the trees and arranged for their contribution. On a bitterly cold Saturday, 10 February 1979, Joe Bolduc and his crew cut down the two mature 140-foot pines in Fremont, New Hampshire. Only a dozen observers watched the beginning of life for the vessel, but Michael Gowell began his 16mm. documentary film that day.[17]

Reduced to four big logs about 40 feet long, the pines were hauled by truck to Strawbery Banke during late April. There a skilled crew, including Ellis Rowe of Wells, Maine, Robert Simpson of York,

Knees of the Captain Adams *attached to chine logs with view extending to uncompleted bow. PGP.*

Maine, and Robert Eger of Dover, began shaping them into chine logs. Armed with the Smithsonian Institution plans of the *Fanny M.*, Bud McIntosh and William A. Baker served as technical consultants. With the crew swinging broadaxes and adzes, chips flew. The construction site was near the Strawbery Banke boat shop.[18]

According to Al Hickey, "The problem of building the vessel was trying to find those skills and methods which we had a hundred years ago—the materials, the workmen—and produce the same type of craft today." One could not turn back the clock. "We made the compromise in using power tools," Bob Eger said. "It would have been fun to do it in the old way, but the reality of time and money forced us to change that." Otherwise the project would have required three additional years.[19]

The great virgin forests of New England were gone. "The forests are denuded of 70-foot hemlocks," Lew Roberts said. This circumstance created an immediate problem. "We couldn't obtain the same size logs that Adams did." Bob Eger said. "I hunted for the right trees, but it was mainly time-consuming and non-productive. The word was around that we wanted trees. Generally we alerted loggers to be on the lookout for them." The State of New Hampshire lent its support in this search,

The finding, cutting, and shaping of crooked limbs required much time and effort. Bud McIntosh, (above left) pointing to a satisfactory limb on an oak overhanging his Dover Point shop. PGP. Ellis Rowe, (above right) displaying the curvature of finished bow plank. Bob LaPree photo, NHT. Robert Eger (below) checking the square edge of a hackmatack knee for final shaping. Bob LaPree photo. NHT.

but the situation was a tree here and a couple of trees there, a piecemeal collection.[20]

Hackmatack or larch trees, used for the gundalow's knees, were the most difficult to obtain. Found in bogs where it puts out heavy spreading roots, the hackmatack provides naturally grown crooks for structural support of the boat. The knees of the gundalow required an angle of 110 degrees. The more knots in the wood the tougher it is. Frank Morse of Cherryfield, Maine, is virtually the only supplier in the country for these special trees. Now eighty-five years old and still working ten hours a day in season, Morse has seventy years of experience in the trade.[21]

"Frank Morse has orders ahead for ten years with his hackmatack trees." said Mrs. Irene Stivers, a Project committee member. "We went through the Mystic Seaport Museum and they allowed six knees they had ordered from Morse to come directly to us. In the old days, they had regular lots to grow hackmatack trees." Now Mrs. Stivers was compelled to advertise for trees in newspapers, to send out letters soliciting them, and to telephone prospective suppliers. Ex-Governor Sherman Adams of Lincoln, a leading New Hampshire lumberman, joined in the search. "I telephoned him weekly at one point," Mrs. Stivers said. "But his search was to no avail."[22]

The Great Search continued: for "old-growth pine trees capable of yielding top-grade planking, 'hackmatack' or larch trees suitable for knees, locust for trunnels, oak for beams, and pine trunks with a curve ...for bow and stern timbers, or 'sweeps.'" Demonstrating that Captain Adams's renowned "eye for crooked wood" endured in the region, Jack Adams, a UNH photographer, spotted several bent pines in 1980 on a bank of the Bellamy River. Bud McIntosh was called in to examine the trees. "The curve is right," Bud said. Tom Wilson, the owner of the property, donated the trees to the Project. Others scouted the woods in Berwick and Ossipee for hackmatack. Maynard Bray of Brooklin, Maine, an expert on old-time shipbuilding, volunteered to search his part of the state and to coordinate with Frank Morse. In Bray's words, hackmatacks would have to "have enough meat on them" for trimming for the wide angle between the arms.[23]

In July 1980, excitement ran high at the project site. Ellis Rowe felt "like a man who had found buried treasure or inherited money from a distant relative." John Hallett and a diver recovered a cache of rare live oak timbers and knees which had been submerged in a fresh water pond at the Portsmouth Naval Shipyard since 1931. Originally intended

Straddled on the bow, Robert Eger making a head on a trunnel, preparatory to driving a wedge to fasten the bow section. PGP.

as spare wooden parts for "Old Ironsides" and the *USS Constellation.*, the wood was declared surplus by the Navy in the 1950s. After Bob Simpson cut through the muck-covered timber, Rowe and Simpson took a close look and a deep whiff of the smelly wood. It looked beautiful, but after it was dried out, it was found to have heart rot. "It was all silted up and rotted," Bob Eger said, kicking the worthless log, "and we never used it."[24]

Other efforts fared better. In 1979 John P. "Bud" Shevenell of Exeter found a trunnel-making machine gathering dust in his recently acquired boatyard at Boothbay Harbor, Maine. A trunnel was made by running a narrow block of wood through a lathe apparatus. Loaned to the Project, the machine, a rarity today, turned out the 5000 trunnels needed to fasten the gundalow.

The effort to obtain a sail was also successful. "There was a photograph of the *Fanny M.* under full sail," Al Hickey said, "and fortunately the sun shone through it. So we blew up the photograph and were able to determine its dimensions in proportion, the various threads, brails, and stitching. We contacted a number of sailmakers, and finally selected Nat Wilson, a sailmaker of East Boothbay, Maine, as the person most receptive to our plans. He made it to order." Again a sensible compromise with the past was struck. "The old sails were pure cotton and wouldn't last long," Lew Roberts said. "It would have rotted away within a few years." The Project directors obtained a 1080-square foot duck mainsail treated with Barfair/Vivatex to assure durability.[25]

As the materials were being assembled, Ellis Rowe and his men went to work. A bearded barrel-chested man originally from North Carolina, Rowe was experienced in boatbuilding at his own yard in Wells, but this job was bigger than usual. The crew first built the hull, and then the decking, an aft cabin, and the mast arrangement. "It has been by far the largest boat I have worked on," David Gebow, a ship's carpenter, said. "It takes two or three people to move the logs. We are physically tired at the end of the day." The 69-foot, 45 ton vessel has a bow slightly larger than the stern and is shaped like a codfish. The time and money involved in building a gundalow has drastically changed. "When the boats were in vogue," Bud McIntosh said, "a gundalow might cost $3000 and take eight months to construct." The original estimate in 1978 was that construction would require eighteen months at a cost of $50,000 to $60,000. Inflation raised that figure as fast as an incoming Piscataqua tide.[26]

An estimate in 1980 projected the increase necessary to complete the job: $17,594.44 for additional materials and 4704 man hours required to do the work. With every passing day, the crew appreciated more the efforts of the old-timers and viewed their job as "an educational experience." Bob Simpson made the oars or "sweeps," measuring forty-two feet long. In a formal application, the Project directors asked the *Guinness Book of World Records* to recognize the oar as the world's longest. (The *Guinness* editors informed the Project that there was no category for oars.) During the winter in the "off season," there was no rest. Bob Eger completed several important pieces, including the leeboard and rudder.[27]

The extensive ironwork, including the sweeplocks and sheet horse, was forged at Peter Happny's blacksmith shop in Portsmouth. Leaving the family farm in Candia, Happny became interested in smithing while an engineering student at UNH. After working as the Strawbery Banke blacksmith, Happny started his own business. In his shop, with classical music playing in the background, Happny forged the rudder and leeboard bands. He reinforced the main sheethorse over the cuddy with diagonal bracing. For parts which would be under water, he used wrought iron; for those above water, he selected steel. In his craft, Happny has made adjustments to modern times. "The old-timers used a punch," he said. "I use a drill for holes in wrought iron." The 18th century blacksmith had charcoal for his forge, but "I use coal for a hotter fire." When he opened his shop, Happny relied on bellows. "Pumping bellows 70,000 times a year," he said, "didn't do anything for my humor." He now uses a blower powered by an electric motor.[28]

As construction proceeded, several controversies developed over the gundalow's design. The many models, drawings, and sets of measurements of the *Fanny M.* rarely agreed. During 1980 the issue of the extent of flare arose as an adjunct to the finding of the knees. The 1937 Taylor drawings, based upon 1925 Wilkes' measurements, showed a flare of about 115 degrees (the angle formed by the bottom planking and the side planking.) Bud McIntosh believed the size of this angle was exaggerated, saying that gundalows were nearly straight-sided.

To resolve this dilemma, the builders, along with McIntosh, Charles Powers from the Newburyport boat yard, and several Project directors, met at the Portsmouth Athenaeum to examine the Gordon Wilkes model. Illness prevented the appearance of William A. Baker. The conferees decided the Wilkes model was probably accurate and copied the 102 degree angle for the flare on the *Adams*. It was hypothesized by those in attendance that the flare in the Taylor drawings resulted from his acceptance of the Wilkes measurements from a hull which had lost her shape on the Dover Point beach. In this rotted state, the hull had probably sprung outward by the time Wilkes took his lines in 1925. The group also examined the Clyde Whitehouse models at the Old Berwick Historical Society, and later considered some notes and measurements by Whitehouse which had been discovered in the meantime. The Whitehouse source indicated a flare of 106 degrees. The issue was resolved, with a little debate, to rely upon the 102 degree figure, which, given the conflicting evidence, seemed reasonable. Thus the beam of the *Adams* is less than that of the *Fanny M.*, as represented by Taylor.

Another controversy occurred during the same year. Its origins lay in the construction of the ends. As Captain Adams was able to find large bow logs, he could do much more shaping than his modern counterparts at Strawbery Banke yard. Rowe and Eger were compelled to work with twenty smaller pieces, as opposed to the ten or twelve which

View of the bow of the nearly completed Captain Adams *with Sampson mast. PGP.*

Adams used for the same section. Eger said,

> As we neared the sides of the hull, we were unable to follow those [Taylor's] lines because we didn't have timbers of adequate size. What we did was not to bring the outer bow logs back as sharply as the Taylor drawings suggested. However, a meeting at the gundalow with William A. Baker brought out his disagreement with our solution to the problem. At his behest we removed the outer bow logs and brought them back more sharply. We accomplished this by adding extra pieces of wood to the inside of the outer bow logs.[29]

The construction of the stern followed the same pattern of trying to devise a reasonable compromise amidst so much conflicting evidence. The builders started working on the stern, following the lines of the Taylor drawings as much as the material allowed. A dispute arose when it was seen that the *Adams* would have corners at the stern where the *Fanny M.* had softer curves. At a meeting, the same people involved in the earlier conferences discovered the various models and drawings had four different lines to represent the same curve. It was out of the question to tear down the timbers of the *Adams*, weakening her in the process, to try to produce a more gradual curve as some proposed. This alternative would have involved a major reconstruction of the stern, using built-up pieces as had been done for the bow. The final decision on this matter allowed the builders to soften the curve as much as possible, given the construction already completed.

"This course perhaps resulted in the *Captain Adams*," Bob Eger said, "being a less perfect replica of the *Fanny M*. In my opinion, it resulted in a more authentic gundalow construction being led by available materials and expedience rather than a more abstract idea of proper lines." This appraisal found common agreement. "No one was completely happy with the decision," Peggy Armitage said. "But Bud McIntosh reminded them that there never were two gundalows exactly alike as earlier builders seldom worked, if ever, from blueprints." This final outcome is fitting, since Captain Adams never used plans, and the gundalow was a haphazardly built vessel at best.[30]

Caulking and Outfitting the Vessel

Caulking the vessel was a time-consuming and expensive process. Some $5000 to $6000 was allocated for this work. Barry Hayes, Edward Jalbert, and Andrew Johnson devoted an entire spring to the critical and extensive sealing operation.

The first step was to insert a layer of cotton between the seams with a caulking or "making" iron. Then the caulkers twisted long flat oakum (hemp treated with a special oil) into rope-like thickness. "Rippling" the oakum, they doubled its thickness by overlapping and bunching it together. But one layer is not enough. They tapped in a second strand of oakum. It was important to follow a system to know which seams had been caulked. After completing the butts of the hull, the caulkers worked on the horizontal seams. "One leaves an end or a 'tail' sticking out, which indicates where the end of the caulking is," Jalbert said. "When one sees two tails, he knows it is complete."[31]

The caulkers were watchful for other things. "If the wood is wedged tight together," Barry Hayes said, "it is necessary to pry it apart with a 'dumb' iron to insert the necessary caulking. Otherwise the boat would have a slow leak." When the caulking was finished, the crew applied red lead paint, which seals and hardens the oakum and fills in the seam. To assure an even surface, they smoothed putty over the caulked seams. Centuries ago, builders used pine tar, direct from the trees. When the boat was in the water, the swelling of the wood combined with the cotton, oakum, paint, and putty, would tighten and seal the cracks.[32]

Three men caulking produced an intense cacophony. The caulkers wore protective ear muffs. Visitors strolling in the area would approach to a certain point and then stop when the noise hurt their ears. "People who live nearby in the area," Jalbert remarked good–naturedly, "told us to start a little later than 6:00 A.M., as they were awakened by the noise."[33]

When Ellis Rowe left as the supervising chief builder of the gundalow to work on another boat, Bob Eger assumed the responsibility of the construction of the *Adams*. Amidst his many duties, Eger turned his attention to finding a spruce for the seventy-foot spar. He found the log, not in the woods, but already cut and shaped for this purpose at Rockland, Maine. Eger located what he was looking for stored outside on blocking. (The tree has been cut several years before at Ashland, Maine.) After completely restoring the *J. and E. Riggin*, a windjammer schooner, by 1977, Dave and Sue Allen had used this spruce as a mainmast for two or three years. Replacing it with a Douglas Fir from the Pacific Northwest, the Allens had no further use for their original Maine spar. They sold it to the Project at a bargain price. When the log arrived at Strawbery Banke on 24 April 1982, Eger with some help from Stephen Brake reshaped the spar to meet the specifications of the *Adams*. After four coats of linseed oil to its shaved surface, the 69-foot, 11-inch pole took on a golden hue.[34]

The Project directors instructed the builders to insure the boat's long life with structural reinforcements, preservatives, and care to do the job right. The old timers were often satisfied to build for the short-term, but the *Adams*, for use as an educational exhibit, was built to withstand the ravages of time. "It should last for fifty years," Bud McIntosh predicted. "The gundalow is, in fact, overbuilt," Lew Roberts said. "We took many more pains with it compared with the old farmers. There should be very little maintenance on it." According to Steve Brake, a ship's carpenter and a student at a boatbuilding school in Eastport, Maine,

> The problem with the boat in the future will be water condensation inside. There it is quite hot, and moisture collects. The interior is treated with linseed oil diluted with kerosene,which will soak rapidly and spread into the wood. This application will be kept up and the inside watched to prevent early rot. The outside of the boat is painted more for the sake of cosmetics.[35]

For a long time, the Building Committee of the Project and Bob Eger pondered about the exterior color of the gundalow. Eger finally decided to paint the hull barn red, a color often used by the old-timers. Below the waterline and covering the bottom of the boat, he applied a russet-brown antifouling paint. This special preservative, developed in modern times and unknown to the old gundalow builders, discourages the encrustation of barnacles and activity of borers.

In season, the construction site was a busy place, as the crew worked on the gundalow while local people, visitors, and tour groups watched. By 1982 the *Adams* was taking on her final form, with the addition of the rudder, tiller, wheel, and cutwater. Amidst all their activity, Eger and his crew answered questions and heard reminiscences about the old days. Some remembered Captain Adams.

The nearby storage building on Whidden Place provided both a tool shed upstairs and a pilot exhibit on the ground floor. The exhibit featured photographs, charts, a scale model by James McReynolds and memorabilia associated with the gundalow era, the Piscataqua Basin and Captain Adams. Items included a tide scale and the machine used to make the 5000 trunnels. On the grounds, a 12-foot eeling punt built in 1898 by Thomas Davidson of New Castle, and owned by Captain Adams, attracted the sightseer's attention. Restored and donated by Ned Ackerman, the antique brought memories to Bud McIntosh, who recalled the punt when it was fully sheathed inside "to keep the eels from getting stuck under the ribs."[36]

Visitors also saw Peter Happny at work. Using his portable forge, Happny hot-riveted the leeboard band at the construction site. He installed the other ironwork he had made at his shop. "These pieces are so structured," Happny said, "I won't have to worry about repairing them in my lifetime."[37]

The Last Months

During the winter of 1981 – 1982, many expressed doubt that the gundalow would be launched in time to celebrate the 250th anniversary of the founding of Durham on 26 June. By early 1982, the total cost of construction and displaying the boat had jumped from the original estimate of $50,000 to between $80,000 and $90,000. To overcome this financial crisis, the Project needed $25,000. But the uncertain future for the partially completed gundalow did not discourage Irene Stivers. "I'm an optimist," she said. "I would like to push it [the gundalow] all the way, if necessary," People in Durham would be "extremely disappointed if we can't make it, and so would I."[38]

All outside construction came to a complete standstill that winter. Without funds, the work could not resume in the spring. William A. Baker, friend and advisor to the Project, had died suddenly in September 1981. The prospect was gloomy. "The five-year history of the Piscataqua Gundalow Project would make a fitting sequel to the 'Perils of Pauline,'" Albert Hickey wrote in the *Piscataqua Current* newsletter. "Time after time since its inception, the Project directors have looked at a close-to-zero bank balance and asked, 'Shall we go for it...or shall we fold it?'"[39]

The Project directors went for it. The Wheelabrator-Frye Corporation had contributed $6200 over the years, and other donors gave generously. But the Project still needed additional funds.[40]

The Congoleum Corporation of Portsmouth rose to the occasion. In 1981, they had given $2500. The officers of the company were perhaps drawn by a previous association: the first local office of Congoleum was housed in the historic Cotton House, overlooking the Strawbery Banke construction site. Encouraged by the earlier donation, Richard Gallant decided to approach Congoleum again. To do this, Gallant saw Peter Rice. Prominent in Portsmouth business circles, Rice knew Byron Radaker, the chairman of Congoleum, and was glad to arrange a meeting. In February 1982, the three men met to discuss the matter. Radaker pledged $25,000 in a five-year, interest-free loan. The Project directors put up the unfinished gundalow as collateral. The Project was saved.[41]

Although the financial battle had been won, final victory still seemed a long way off. Arrangements for launching the yet uncompleted vessel and various legal matters had to be resolved in a race to beat the June 26th deadline. Although Bob Eger and his crew returned to work on March 1st, their first week was frustrating. "I've been shoveling snow," Eger said. "After that, I found six inches of water under the boat, the way weather conditions are."

To comply with regulations, the Project officers notified the U.S. Coast Guard authorities in Portland, Maine, about the *Adams*. Since the boat was "not a vessel for hire, and as it was not carrying passengers," the skipper of the vessel would not have to be licensed. The *Adams* was built strictly for educational purposes. As Lew Roberts explained,

The gundalow will carry no passengers, due to U.S. Coast Guard regulations. Otherwise we would have to have life preservers on board and having those and other safety devices prominently displayed would ruin the appearance of the gundalow, and defeat the whole purpose for which it was built. Once it is tied up to a dock, we can invite people aboard, as the safety regulations aren't in effect then.[42]

As spring progressed, institutions and individuals cleaned out their attics and basements, and donated parts for the *Adams*. The New Hampshire Farm Museum donated the ship's wheel. The bilge pump, taken from a barge owned by David Mahoney, was overhauled by Dan O'Reilly. Two old anchors became available; one came from the Kittery Historical and Naval Museum, while the other, once on the "baby" gundalow, was given by Evelyn Browne. Robert Corell procured the original lamp of the *Fanny M.*[43]

Searching for a tree for the stump mast, Bob Eger located a tall white oak growing in the UNH Foss Farm Woodlot. A Forestry Department crew felled the tree. On the ground, it measured eighty feet. A count of its rings indicated the oak was eighty-six years old. The stump mast, cut and shaped to Eger's specifications, is 21 feet long and is 14 inches in diameter.

One major problem remaining for the Project officials and Eger's crew was the moving of the *Adams* from her construction site across a field and a paved street to the Piscataqua River about a quarter mile distant. Once the boat arrived there, provisions had already been made for its berthing. In 1980 the City Council of Portsmouth granted the Project the use of Sheafe Warehouse for various gundalow models, tools, and artifacts. This gesture was historically significant since the warehouse, built by Jacob Sheafe in 1705, was actually used by the gundalows docking at the Sheafe Wharf. The Sheafe Warehouse, a three-story structure with a gabled end overhanging the water from which gundalows were loaded and unloaded, was available as a docking berth for the *Adams*, just as it would have been in earlier Portsmouth history. In 1982, the land adjacent to the warehouse was purchased and a portion made available to the Project. This site afforded an even better docking facility for the *Adams*.

The Project officers decided to employ oxen to pull the vessel, the traditional method in times past. The initial move to transport the gundalow most of the way was scheduled for Monday, June 7 , followed by

Pulling of the Captain Adams *by oxen teams across a soggy Strawbery Banke field in June 1982. The oxen were driven by their owners, Conrad Small of York, Maine, and Frank Scruton of Rochester, New Hampshire. John Bardwell photo. UNHMS.*

Launch Day, June 13, when the gundalow would be pulled the remaining distance to tidewater.

Bob Eger and his crew removed the construction blocks and, using jacks, lowered the *Adams* to a bed of rollers. Rain or shine, the oxen would be there. Eger's crew would be ready at 8:00 A.M., but the oxen would not be on the job until 10:00 A.M. "They belong to the union," one of the crew said.

The Launching of the Adams

Almost continuous rain and drizzle for three days cancelled the scheduled oxen pull on Monday, June 7. The field was a swamp. Finally the storm passed out to sea, and Tuesday, June 8, brought the sun drying up the mire. Bob Eger and his crew, along with volunteers, laid log poles at intervals in front of the bow of the *Adams*, in anticipation of the oxen.

Conrad Small of York, Maine arrived with his six oxen and yoked them up. One of them, five-year old Tom, was billed as "probably the largest ox in New England," and weighed in at 3800 pounds. Frank Scruton came over from his Rochester dairy farm with Babe and Broad, two massive white oxen. These eight beasts were more accustomed to county fair pulls and tasks around the farm than to this assignment. "This is the way they used to haul gundalows in the old days," Scruton said. "When they asked us to come over and help out, we were happy to do it. It's kind of fun for us—something different."[44]

By mid-morning, a large crowd of well-wishers had gathered to watch the event. Strawbery Banke officials held the crowd back while Small, Scruton and their assistants readied their teams. The oxen yokes were attached to a cable which reached to a rigging on the gundalow's bow. The cable looped around a deadman, in this case a stout tree trunk on the edge of the Banke parking lot.

"Gee up! Gee up! Gee up!" the drovers yelled frenziedly, cracking their whips repeatedly on the backs and shoulders of the oxen. The beasts dug their hooves into the turf. They plodded forward. The cable pulled taut. The gundalow slid ahead on its log rollers. "Whoa! Whoa! Whoa!" the drovers yelled as the gundalow approached the end of the logs. With tongs and peaveys the crew brought the rear logs to the front in preparation for another pull. Doesn't that hurt the oxen?" asked a worried little girl. "It's cruel," her anguished friend said. But the oxen were unharmed.

Pulls continued into the late afternoon. Sometimes the gundalow swerved almost off the poles. At one place, Eger's crew had to lay planks across a soggy stretch of the field to prevent the poles from being driven into the muck. Despite these setbacks, the work went on. By the end of the afternoon, the gundalow was resting on the hard ground of the Banke's Dunaway Store parking lot, within striking distance of the river. The next objective was moving across the road into Prescott Park.

The Marconi property, which had split Prescott Park, was purchased by Joseph Sawtelle to advance the interests of the historic waterfront and the park. The land was obtained as well for its pier which afforded a superb docking facility for the gundalow. In anticipation of the gundalow move, the fences were taken down to form one continuous park, and the open land provided free access. Trucks brought in load after load of fill, whereupon bulldozers graded down the surface and removed any rocks. Renovating the dock, carpenters replaced unsafe planks.

Thursday, June 10 was another move day, but this time it was conducted without oxen. The problem was to haul the gundalow across Marcy Street as quickly as possible to Prescott Park without disrupting traffic on that busy street. Since oxen cannot dig in to pavement, they would have floundered awkwardly. To assure a speedy, if historically inaccurate, move across the street, Dick Gallant brought over his ancient red truck from Newmarket.

With all obstacles removed, Gallant's truck winched the boat across the road. The route of the gundalow passed over a corner of Prescott Park, and entered Sawtelle's land on an angle. To prevent any damage to the gundalow's rudder during the launch, the vessel was turned completely around so that the stern could enter the water first. If the *Adams* had been rigged up before this mechanically powered move, the 69-foot yard and stump mast would not have cleared the telephone and power lines. These items, along with the leeboard, were accordingly transported separately.[45]

Rain was forecast and gray skies hovered over Portsmouth on Sunday, June 13. Despite the threat of bad weather, the launching had to proceed as planned to adhere to the timetable for assuring the gundalow's arrival at Durham on June 26. The spring high tide would occur at 5:06 P.M. on this gloomy Sunday. By noon a crowd had gathered. The crew hauled up the stump mast on deck with pullies and installed it upright. Lewis Roberts attached an American flag with thirteen stars to the mast as Robert Corell steadied the ladder. The skies darkened. The Nonesuch Morris dancers from Durham presented their old English dances on deck.

At 2:30 P.M., the rain came, a pelting cold rain under which the crowd brought out umbrellas and yellow slickers. Eger's crew stood under the branches of a nearby tree, munching hamburgers. They were feeling the pressure of the launch schedule. "We've worked every day," Steve Brake said, "for fourteen days straight."

The oxen of Conrad Small and Frank Scruton, five team or ten animals on this occasion, were yoked up. This time the oxen faced inland and opposite the gundalow, as the deadman through which the cable was secured was located behind the five teams. At about 4:30 P.M., with the rain still falling, the oxen planted their hooves in the mud and moved ahead. The crowd, estimated at about three thousand, cheered wildly. People stood in lines four and five deep along the sides of the gundalow. Others leaned forward from the railing on the dock, or out the windows of the Sheafe Warehouse. Yachts, sailboats, and dories maintained their favored positions on the river. Several pulls over the

Amidst the rain, the crew of the Captain Adams *awaiting the final pull to launch the vessel in the tidewater of the Piscataqua on 13 June 1982. Oxen teams on left. The Portsmouth Naval Shipyard across the river in background. Douglas Armsden photo. DAC.*

planks and poles brought the *Adams* to the edge of the bank. Only one more was necessary to topple the gundalow down the embankment into the tidewater.

At 5:00 P.M., the oxen and their drovers paused. On deck the Board of Trustees of the Project, many of whom were contributing their physical labor for the launch, the regular crew, and various dignitaries gave their attention to John Hallett, acting as master of ceremonies. Hallett grasped the wet microphone. "The gundalow is one of the vessels," Hallet said, "which made Portsmouth and the Piscataqua River Basin a great place." Robert Corell, bareheaded, his face dripping with water, thanked the many people who contributed their time and money to this undertaking. "Al Hickey had a dream," Corell said, "and finally it has come true." Ada Lundholm, grand-niece of Captain Adams,

As the stern of the Adams *hits the water during her launch, Lewis Roberts, with his hand holding the helmswheel, smiling happily. Robert Corell, standing in white pants below flag. Sheafe Warehouse on left. Ralph Morang photo. HU.*

christened the vessel on the bow cutwater with a bottle of water taken from the Great Bay at Adams Point.[46]

"Please clear the dock," Lewis Roberts and Corell repeatedly warned. "This is for your own safety." Finally the people relinquished their prime viewing stations and moved off an extension of the pier just outside the path in which the gundalow was headed. The oxen pulled. Those on deck held onto the yard, wheel, or sheet horse. It was 5:30 P.M.

The *Adams* tumbled off her perch and slid down the embankment amidst the cheers and applause of onlookers and the tooting of boats' horns. With a great splash, the vessel hit the water. Veering unexpectedly, the gundalow slammed into the pier, making an audible "crunch." The collision ripped out a piling and cracked several timbers. The platform where people had been standing moments before sagged. The gundalow bounced clear and came to rest along the dock. "There were some hitches and starts and the whole thing probably took us twice as long as it should have," Hallett said. "But it's been a long time since anyone did this sort of thing, and we're all sort of amateurs."[47]

The Great Splash was over, probably the first gundalow launch on the Piscataqua in ninety years. Most spectators left immediately, but some lingered to take photographs or shout congratulations to the crew.

Bob Eger and his men first secured the vessel to the dock. Then they passed around a victory bottle of wine. All had worked on this boat for months, years in Bob's case. They shared the mutual mishaps of cut fingers and thumbs, bumped heads, delays in the arrival of materials and attendant problems. Eger occasionally awoke in the middle of the night to wonder if he would ever finish the vessel on time. Bob and one or two others would remain with the *Adams* during the summer to complete the interior work and other finishing touches. But with the exhaustion of the Project's construction funds, most of the crew were leaving within a few days. Some planned to work at other boatyards up and down the New England coast.

The Voyage to Durham

For the next ten days, the *Adams* remained at the dock. A sump pump was installed in the cuddy to remove water. Despite the swelling of the hull, a geyser spouted through a crack along a seam. To repair this leak, a diver went below the hull and shoved sawdust into the right place. The force of the geyser sucked the sawdust up the crack and plugged the hole for the time being.

A sunny hot day finally broke the spell of rainy weather for the cruise up the Piscataqua on Thursday, 24 June. Aboard the *Adams*, the regular crew members, some Project officials and others, totalling about twenty, were ready for the 11:30 A.M. incoming tide. Irene Stivers was appointed honorary captain. The McIntosh brothers, thirty years after their launching of the *Driftwood*, were back on the job. Ned McIntosh joined the group on the *Adams*. Aboard the tug *William Badger* of New Castle, owned by Daniel Tarbell, Bud McIntosh, Tarbell, and Cyrus Sweet were assigned the responsibility of towing the *Adams* up to Durham. As the rigging and sail had not yet been installed, Dick Gallant's dream of sailing the gundalow up the Piscataqua on its maiden voyage was dashed. A crowd on the repaired dock gave an enthusiastic send-off.

The gundalow in tandem to the *William Badger* was under way at 11:45 A.M. A number of escort boats—*Sagamore*, *Heritage*, a U.S. Coast Guard auxiliary ship, and two or three other vessels—followed the *Adams* at a safe distance. The drawbridge operator raised the middle section of the Portsmouth Memorial Bridge to permit the *Adams* to pass safely underneath. With flawless towing and the incoming tide, the gundalow made a fast trip up the river past the familiar landmarks: Pulpit Rock, the Long Reach, the Horseraces, Bloody Point, Dover Point, Goat Island, Little Bay, and Fox Point. The trip went so effortlessly that the boat outran the tide. It was necessary to await the incoming water.

In a fitting gesture, the gundalow anchored off Adams Point for forty-five minutes in view of the site of the Adams homestead and the fields surrounding the tomb. During the wait, Andy Johnson, a crew member, grew restless. Without telling anyone of his intentions, he climbed up on the slung yard, walked carefully with one barefoot step after the other to the yard's end, and dove into the Great Bay. The Skipper had always liked unexpected boyish pranks, and would have joined in with the cheers of those observing the feat.

Coming aboard the *William Badger*, Herbert Jackson, the long-time pilot for the Oyster River, guided the tug for the rest of the voyage. There was no problem at the Half Tide Rock at the mouth of the river; this rock, actually more of an extended ledge with paint of many scraped boat bottoms adorning it, was now safely under water at full tide. Jackson piloted his craft through the red and black tipped sapling stakes, still cut and placed anew by volunteers every spring to mark the channel after the ice breaks up. Wagon Hill, Jackson's Landing, and finally General Sullivan's house atop the riverbank came into view. At 3:35 P.M. in the bright sun, the *Adams* arrived at the Durham Town Landing. The whole voyage went "as smooth as silk," Ned McIntosh said. On shore a few hundred spectators and a band provided an impromptu celebration. The gundalow had come home.

At 11:00 A.M. on Saturday, June 26, a crowd of about a thousand people gathered at the Durham Town Landing. The *Adams* lay beached on the low-tide mud, listing toward the channel. Dressed as Colonel James Davis, Durham's moderator in 1732, Joseph Michael, who now held the same position, re-convened the town meeting which he had opened earlier at the Durham Community Church. Rain had driven that part of the program for Durham's 250th anniversary of the founding of the town to indoor quarters, but now the sky was clearing.

Lewis Roberts, appearing in a blue suit in vivid contrast to his deckhand's garb a week before, presented the gundalow to the townspeople. "It is fitting," Roberts said, "that the first town the gundalow is visiting honors a native son, as Captain Adams came from Durham

On her maiden voyage under tow, the Adams *docking at the Durham Town Landing on Oyster River at high tide on 24 June 1982. Alan Klehr photo. PGP.*

Point." As if to dramatize the passage of time between the early days of Durham which the replica represented and the present age, a jet from Pease Air Force Base at Newington roared overhead to drown out Roberts's words. After the noise subsided, he began again. "A few days ago, a young girl asked me about the leeboard," Roberts said. "She wanted to know, 'Are you going to raise the door and let the oxen in?'"[48]

     "People have asked me," he continued, "'Can we take the gundalow out for a cruise?' According to Coast Guard regulations, you would need a motor and radar on the stump mast, and the boat would lose the total authenticity for which it was built." After Roberts presented a trunnel for display at the Durham Town Hall, the Nonesuch Morris dancers performed, invoking good luck and prosperity for the crops and the gundalow. With a reading of a special poem written for the occasion and a singing of the "Star Spangled Banner," Michael adjourned the town meeting which would re-convene "fifty years from now."

Cruises into the Future

The influence of the *Captain Edward H. Adams* is already evident in the Piscataqua region. Brown traffic signs, with the likeness of a gundalow, appear at highway exits and street intersections to direct travelers to the berthing site of the *Adams*. The word "gundalow," obscure for so many years, now brings instant recognition for an increasing number of people in the area. "You don't have to explain to people in Durham anymore what the word means," said Sharon Meeker, the UNH docent coordinator.[49]

An application to the National Endowment for the Humanities in late 1981 for a $217,950 grant to implement the educational program was not approved. But encouraged by its overall reception by NEH officials, Robert Corell will submit a revised application.

In the meantime, plans to use the gundalow as a catalyst for the educational program are moving ahead. "We'll gear the display to the local town history and situation," Sharon Meeker said. "The emphasis for Newmarket, for example, will be on its mills. The town also has a colonial-style militia regiment [the Newmarket Militia], to re-enact their role during the Revolution."

"For small groups, especially children," Meeker continued, we can take them down into the cuddy, and present a slide show. On deck we can present children's plays. People in costumes will act out their historical roles, a fisherman, a worker at a brickyard or a lady schoolteacher. A girl working in a Newmarket mill might board a gundalow to hitch a ride to Portsmouth for a weekend home.

For adults, the program will emphasize the modern concerns of the Piscataqua basin: the ecology, water resources, recreational uses, population growth, and so forth. The deck of the gundalow is quite large, and can be used as a stage for lectures, plays, and concerts.[50]

The educational program is intended to bring improvements to the estuary and restore the waterfront to its former prominence. Piscataqua towns, whose most historic areas are their waterfronts, will benefit from public understanding of the history of the river and its current problems and potential.

After the *Adams* is made shipshape during the summer and fall of 1982, the gundalow will be a busy vessel from May to October. In the years ahead the *Adams* is tentatively scheduled to appear at a

After six years of planning and work and $100,000 in costs, the dream became a reality. The Adams *under sail for the first time on her voyage from Durham to Portsmouth in Piscataqua waters during July 1982. Douglas Armsden photo. DAC.*

number of town celebrations and events. These ports of call include not only the Piscataqua Basin but also such nearby coastal communities as York, Maine and Hampton, New Hampshire. If plans materialize, sound and light dramas will be presented at several ports, including the Sheafe Warehouse and also the Hamilton House (ca. 1730) in South Berwick, Maine, the setting of Sarah Orne Jewett's *The Tory Lover* (1901). The script will be adopted from the novel. At Exeter, the *Adams* will appear as a prop in a play depicting the arrival of General Sullivan in a gundalow bearing barrels of gunpowder taken in the 1774 Fort William and Mary raid.[51]

For two and a half centuries, the gundalow performed an outstanding job as a cargo bearer. Brought back to life in a different role and set of circumstances, she is being called upon to undertake another important mission. In the years to come, the *Captain Edward H. Adams* will serve as a bearer of education and information to Piscataqua citizens.

Bon voyage.

Footnotes

Footnotes for the Introduction

1. Taylor, "Survey #171," reprinted as pp. 127–139, 209–222; Saltonstall, pp. 180–191; Klewin, pp. 32–37.
2. Dennett interview.
3. Dudley interview.
4. Clark interview.
5. Blaisdell, pp. 17–19; Wilcomb, pp. 21–23.
6. Baker, 1: 82–83.
7. C. Clark, pp. 159–161; Bourne, pp. 529–530.
8. Ordway, pp. 249–263.
9. Merrit, pp. 21–22.
10. Chapelle, *The History of the American Sailing Navy*, pp. 101–114; Norris, pp. 160–165.
11. *New York Times*, 14 February 1982.
12. Crowninshield, pp. 1–4; Kaplan, pp. 330–351.
13. Whittier, p. 401.
14. *Ibid.*, p. 82.
15. Jewett, pp. 9–10.
16. Dudley, pp. 45–53.
17. Roberts, *Northwest Passage*, pp. 37, 40.
18. Roberts, *Rabble in Arms*, pp. 242–243, 359.
19. Barker, pp. 145–153.
20. Raddall, pp. 52, 166–67.

Footnotes for Chapter I

1. Thompson and Winnick, p. 84.
2. Thompson, pp. 195–195; Brighton, 2:3.
3. Whitehouse interview; Bell, p. 1.

4. Hitchcock, 1: 313–314.
5. D. McIntosh interview.
6. *Ibid.*
7. Saltonstall, p. 6.
8. *Ibid.*, pp. 8–9.
9. N. Adams, p. 43.
10. Klewin, p. 33; Taylor, p. 132.
11. Sawyer interview.
12. D. McIntosh interview.
13. Albee, p. 57.
14. Webster's, p. 490.
15. Taylor, pp. 127-128; Whitehouse collection.
16. Saltonstall, pp. 182–184; Taylor, pp. 129–135.
17. Griffiths, 1: 53.
18. William E. Dennett, Kittery, Maine, to Jane Hunt, Kittery, 13 September 1978, letter, Kittery Historical and Naval Museum Papers.
19. Taylor, pp. 130–131.
20. Dennett to Hunt, 13 September 1978, letter, Kittery Historical and Naval Museum Papers.
21. N. Adams, p. 43; Wadleigh, p. 101.
22. Hammond, 17: 661.
23. *Ibid.* 18: 134.
24. Wadleigh, p. 120; Saltonstall, pp. 186–187.
25. Saltonstall, pp. 31, 55–64; Rowe, pp. 49–51.
26. Hammond, 18: 205–207.
27. Bouton, p. 479.
28. Petitions 1747, Box 1, folder 56, New Hampshire Archives; Hammond, 18: 309; 5: 513.
29. *Ibid.*
30. Fitts, pp. 165–189, with petition on p. 172.
31. Brighton, 1: 36; Saltonstall, p. 182.
32. Parsons, pp. 2–3, "Forward" by Joseph P. Copley.
33. Material on the Fort William and Mary raid is voluminous. See Parsons, pp. 1–32; *Historical New Hampshire*, 29, (winter 1974), entire issue; Wilderson, 30:178–202; Mayo, pp. 140–144. This quotation is from Wilderson, p. 186.
34. Wilderson, p. 230.
35. Page, p. 86; Wilderson, pp. 188–189.
36. Brighton, 1: 57; 2: 90.
37. Aykroyd, p. 145.
38. Wilderson, p. 232.
39. Sweet, p. 247.
40. Amory, pp. 205–206.
41. *Ibid.*, pp. 295–296; Brewster, 1: 150–151.
42. Wilderson, p. 232.
43. *Ibid.*, Amory, pp. 206, 296.
44. Wilderson, pp. 192–194, 234.

45. *Ibid.*
46. *Ibid;* Amory, p. 206; Page, p. 88.
47. Brighton, 1: 58.
48. *Ibid.,* p. 64; W. Clark, 2: 633–635.
49. Bouton, 7: 51.
50. Taylor, pp. 209–222.
51. D. McIntosh interview.
52. Taylor, pp. 209–210.
53. Happny interview.
54. *National Fisherman,* February 1978; Wadleigh, p. 189.
55. D. McIntosh interview; J.P. Adams, *Drowned Valley,* p. 143.
56. Whitehouse interview.
57. Taylor, pp. 218–220; Chapelle, *The National Watercraft Collection,* p. 177. Concerning a technicality, Chapelle states: "This sail is sometimes considered a lateen but it is not; it was designed to allow spar and sail to be quickly lowered when passing under bridges."
58. Lovett, pp. 60–72, with quotation on p. 66.
59. Saltonstall, p. 184.
60. Whitehouse, "Gundalows," p. 7, Whitehouse Collection; Klewin, p. 34.
61. Frost, p. 3; Taylor, p. 133.
62. D. McIntosh interview. Story of Captain Edward H. Adams told to McIntosh.
63. Taylor, pp. 134–136; G.W. Browne, 1: 156–165.
64. Fitts, p. 340.
65. Thompson, p. 194.
66. *Ibid.,* pp. 26–27.
67. J.P. Adams, *Drowned Valley,* p. 144.
68. *Ibid;* Scales, *History of Dover New Hampshire,* p. 221.
69. Brewster, 1: 150.
70. Payson and Laighton, pp. 171–173, with quotation on p. 171.
71. Thompson, p. 197.
72. *Ibid.,* city plan between pp. 76–77.
73. Taylor, p. 134; D. McIntosh interview.
74. Lovering, pp. 40–41; Harkness, pp. 56–58, 189.
75. William Chase receipt, 24 May 1824, Chase Papers, Box 5, folder 1.
76. Lovett, pp. 60–66; *Durham Chronicle,* 15 May 1732.
77. *Ibid.,* pp. 68–70.
78. Chase Papers, Box 4. folder 5.
79. J.P. Adams, *Drowned Valley,* "Preface," by Charles E. Clark, pp. ix–xiii.
80. *Ibid.* pp. 108–115.
81. Roberts interview; Whitehouse, "Gundalows," p. 12, Whitehouse Collection; J.P. Adams, *Drowned Valley,* "Preface," p. xii.
82. Stevens, p. 152.
83. Cole, 2: 73–74.
84. Easton and Saltonstall, pp. 326–343; Gambee, pp. 75–76.
85. George, pp. 61–76, 113–116; Harvey, pp. 53–54.
86. Charlton, pp. 193–196; Works Progress Administration, pp. 153–154; Stackpole, pp. 118–122; Wilcox, p. 30.

87. Charlton, pp. 185–190; Stevens, pp. 152–154.
88. Ricker, pp. 1–17; Jewett, p. 10.
89. Works Progress Administration, p. 272.
90. Saltonstall, pp. 117–118.
91. Pickett, pp. iii–iv, 1–116; Aldrich, pp. 33–34.
92. Taylor, p. 131; Sawyer interview.
93. Stevens, p. 152; J. P. Adams, *Drowned Valley*, p. 134.
94. Clyde Whitehouse note cards, Whitehouse Collection.
95. *Ibid.*, Whitehouse, "Gundalows," p. 8.
96. *Ibid.*, p. 4; Whitehouse cards.
97. *Ibid.*
98. *Ibid.*; Klewin, p. 37.
99. Whitehouse cards.
100. J.P. Adams, *Drowned Valley*, p. 134.
101. Whitehouse cards.
102. J.P. Adams, *Drowned Valley*, p. 134; Taylor, p. 129.
103. Fitts, pp. 341–342; George, pp. 115–116; Harlow, pp. 145–146.
104. Scales, *History of Strafford County*, p. 326.
105. *Ibid.*, Harlow, p. 146.
106. Harlow, p. 154.
107. *Ibid.*
108. Squires, 2: 441; Dennett interview.
109. *Portsmouth Herald*, 25 April 1899.
110. Taylor, p. 129; Smith, "Historical Notes: The *Fanny M.*," p. 2, Whitehouse Collection; Whitehouse interview.

Footnotes for Chapter II

1. Georges, p. 9.
2. E. Browne, p. 21.
3. Thompson, p. 7; *Manchester Union-Leader*, 27 November 1933; Bowen, p. 56.
4. E. Browne, pp. 23–24; Taylor, "Survey #171," p. 12. The spelling and dates of the various Adams family members are taken from the Adams tombstone, Adams Point, Durham.
5. D. McIntosh interview; Georges, p. 9.
6. Georges, pp. 12–13; Saltonstall, p. 188; *Foster's Daily Democrat*, 23 October 1950.
7. Johnson interview; Clipping, ca. 1935, folder #181, Box #6, Adams Papers.
8. Georges, pp. 9–10, 12; Browne, Johnson, and D. McIntosh interviews.
9. Taylor, p. 222.
10. Diary, Box #6, Adams Papers.
11. *Ibid.*; E. McIntosh interview.
12. Johnson interview; folder #173, Box #6, Adams Papers.
13. E. Browne, p. 20; Johnson interview.
14. E. Browne, pp. 24–25; D. McIntosh interview.
15. E. Browne, pp. 25–26.

16. Diary for 1930, Box #6, Adams Papers.
17. *Ibid.*, Johnson interview.
18. D. McIntosh interview; *Foster's Daily Democrat*, 11 August, 1978; "Dover Rotary Notes," 19 July 1978, Whitehouse Collection.
19. Clipping, folder 184, Adams Papers; E. Browne, pp. 26, 40, *Transcript*, 22 February 1981.
20. William G. Saltonstall, Marion Massachusetts, to Richard E. Winslow, Portsmouth, letter, 15 January 1982; Whitehouse interview.
21. Georges p. 11; Johnson interview.
22. Folder #169, Box #6, Adams Papers.
23. *New Hampshire Times*, 10 November 1946.
24. *Ibid.*
25. Clipping, dated 26 June 1948, folder #175, Box #6, Adams Papers; E. Browne, p. 26.
26. Certificate of Death, State of New Hampshire, Concord; *Portsmouth Herald*, 10 April 1951; Bowen, pp. 112–113.
27. Taylor, p. 210; D. McIntosh interview.
28. Taylor, pp. 212–213.
29. *Ibid.*, p. 214.
30. "Gundalows," p. 7, Whitehouse Collection.
31. Taylor, pp. 217–218.
32. *Ibid.*, pp. 221–222.
33. Taylor, "Survey #171," pp. 18–19.
34. *Manchester Morning Union*, 23 October 1950; *Boston Globe*, undated 1936 clipping, folder #175, Box 6, Adams Papers.
35. Taylor, "Survey #171," pp. 34–36.
37. *Ibid.*
38. Bowen, p. 112; Browne interview; J.P. Adams, *Drowned Valley*, p. 243.
39. *Foster's DailyDemocrat*, 23 October 1950; E. McIntosh interview.
40. E. Browne, p. 26; Horgan, photograph and caption, p. 346; Bowen, p. 112.
41. *Ibid; Manchester Morning Union*, 23 October 1950.
42. Sherman Adams, Concord, N.H., to Edward H. Adams, letter, 26 October 1950, folder #168, Box #6, Adams Papers; Dudley interview.
43. E. Browne, pp. 41–42; *Portsmouth Herald*, 25 July 1959.
44. *Foster's Daily Democrat*, 7 July 1981; J.P. Adams, *Drowned Valley*, pp. 242–243; Browne and E. McIntosh interviews.
45. Bowen, p. 113.
46. *Ibid; Portsmouth Herald*, 12 November 1968.
47. *Foster's Daily Democrat*, 7 July 1981; Quackenbush, p. 2.
48. J.P. Adams, *Drowned Valley*, p. 242.

Footnotes for Chapter III

1. Gallant interview.
2. Hickey interview; Hickey *Vita*, folder #1, Project Papers.
3. Hickey, Portsmouth, to Arnold Whittaker, Stratham, 23 January 1978, letter, folder #1, Project Papers; Hickey interview.

4. Armitage interview.
5. Corell interview.
6. Corell memo, 29 September 1977, folder #1, Project Papers.
7. Corell, Durham, to Bruce Miller, Durham, 16 November 1977, letter, folder #1, Project Papers.
8. Gallant interview; folder #1, Project Papers.
9. *Foster's Daily Democrat*, 11 August 1978.
10. "Driftwood" Proposal, folder #1, Project Papers; *Transcript*, 20 July 1982.
11. Charles E. Clark, Durham, to Hickey, Portsmouth, 28 September 1979, letter, folder #2, Project Papers.
12. "Driftwood" Proposal, folder #1, Project Papers; Seeger, pp. 311–312.
13. Dudley and Hickey interviews.
14. Dudley interview.
15. Corell interview.
16. *Portsmouth Herald*, 15 September 1978; Stivers interview.
17. *Foster's Daily Democrat*, 2 March 1979.
18. *Ibid.*, 12 May 1982, Supplement, *Durham Chronicle*, 15 May 1732.
19. Hickey and Eger interviews.
20. Eger and Roberts interviews.
21. Day, pp. 172–175.
22. Stivers interview.
23. *New Hampshire Times*, 20 August 1980; *Piscataqua Current*, January, March 1980.
24. *Portsmouth Herald*, 26 July 1982; Eger interview.
25. *Piscataqua Current*, August 1979; Hickey and Roberts interviews.
26. *Foster's Daily Democrat*, 11 August 1978, 29 July 1980; *York County Coast Star*, 8 July 1981; Gebow interview.
27. *Foster's Daily Democrat*, 4 November 1980; *Piscataqua Current*, August 1980, February 1981.
28. Happny interview.
29. Eger interview.
30. *Ibid.*; Armitage interview.
31. Jalbert interview.
32. *Ibid.*; Hayes interview.
33. *Ibid.*
34. *Portsmouth Herald*, 29 April 1982; *Piscataqua Current*, April 1982; Eger and Brake interviews.
35. Hickey, Newburyport, Massachusetts, to David Gosselin, Hampton, N.H., undated draft letter, ca. 1978, folder #2, Project Papers; Roberts and Brake interviews.
36. NEH Grant Proposal, 13 November 1981, folder #3, Project Papers; *Piscataqua Current*, August 1980, May 1981.
37. *Ibid.*, April 1982.
38. *Foster's Daily Democrat*, 4 January 1982.
39. *Piscataqua Current*, April 1982.
40. *Ibid.*; Vaughn interview.
41. Vaughn and Gallant interviews.

42. Eger and Roberts interviews.
43. *Piscataqua Current*, May 1982.
44. *Foster's Daily Democrat*, 9 June 1982.
45. *Portsmouth Herald*, 29 May 1982.
46. *Ibid.*, 14 June 1982; *Foster's Daily Democrat*, same date.
47. *Ibid.*
48. *Foster's Daily Democrat*, 28 June 1982.
49. Meeker interview.
50. *Ibid.*
51. NEH Grant Proposal, 13 November 1981, folder #3, Project Papers.

Bibliography

My closeness to the subject of this book from an eyewitness vantage point has, indeed, been one of the best sources for this study. A native of the Piscataqua area, I know its history and geography, and I have visited virtually every locale associated with the Piscataqua gundalow story, from Split Rock to the Sheafe Warehouse. I have also been a constant observer of the activities of the Piscataqua Gundalow Project for more than seven months, participating in its meetings, watching the construction of the *Captain Edward H. Adams*, and attending her launching and other events. This opportunity to observe and chronicle history as it is made has enabled me to provide a first-hand historical record of part of the gundalow's story. My account has been supplemented by the following sources:

Books

Adams, John P., *Drowned Valley: The Piscataqua River Basin*. Hanover, N.H.: University Press of New England, 1976.

——, *The Piscataqua River Gundalow*. Durham, N.H.: Printed for the Author, 1982.

Adams, Nathaniel, *Annals of Portsmouth*. Portsmouth: Published by the Author, 1825.

Albee, John, *New Castle: Historic and Picturesque*. Boston: Rand Avery Supply Co., 1884.

Aldrich, Thomas Bailey, *The Story of a Bad Boy*. Boston: Houghton, Mifflin and Co., 1869.

Amory, Thomas C., *The Military Services and Pubic Life of Major-General John Sullivan*. Boston: Wiggin and Lunt, 1868.

Baker, William A., *A Maritime History of Bath, Maine and the Kennebec River Region*. 2 vols. Bath, Maine: Marine Research Society of Bath, 1973.

Barker, Shirley, *The Last Gentleman*. New York: Random House, 1960.

Bell, Charles H., *History of the Town of Exeter, New Hampshire*. Exeter, N.H.: The Quarter-Millennial, 1888.

Blaisdell, Paul H., *Three Centuries on Winnipesaukee*. Somersworth, N.H.: New Hampshire Publishing Co., 1975.

Bourne, Edward E., *The History of Wells and Kennebunk*. Portland, Maine: B. Thurston & Co., 1875.

Brewster, Charles W., *Rambles about Portsmouth*. First Series. Somersworth, N.H.: New Hampshire Publishing Co., 1971. Facsimile of 1873 edition.

Brighton, Raymond A., *They Came to Fish*. 2 vols. Dover, N.H.: Randall/Winebaum Enterprises, 1979.

Chapelle, Howard I., *The History of the American Sailing Navy: The Ships and their Development*. New York: W. W. Norton, & Co., Inc., 1949.

——, *The National Watercraft Collection*. Washington: U.S. Government Printing Office, 1960.

Charlton, Edwin A., *New Hampshire As It Is*. Claremont, N.H.: Tracey and Co., 1856.

Clark, Charles E., *The Eastern Frontier: The Settlement of Northern New England 1610–1763*. New York: Alfred A. Knopf, 1970.

Crowninshield, B. B., *Fore-and-Afters*. Boston: Houghton Mifflin Co., 1940.

Dudley, Albertus T., *The King's Powder*. Boston: Lothrop, Lee & Shepard Co., 1923.

Easton, Howard T., and Saltonstall, William G., eds., *Accounts of Exeter (1750–1800)*. Exeter, N.H.: The News-Letter Press, 1938.

Fitts, James Hill, *History of Newfields, New Hampshire 1638–1911*. Concord, N.H.: The Rumford Press, 1912.

Gambee, Robert, *Exeter Impressions*. New York: Hastings House, 1980.

George, Nellie Palmer, *Old Newmarket*. Exeter, N.H.: The News-Letter Press, 1932.

Griffiths, John W., *The Progressive Ship Builder*. New York: The Nautical Gazette Press, 1875. 2 vols.

Harkness, Marjory Gane, ed., *The Fishbasket Papers; The Diaries, 1768–1823 of Bradbury Jewell, Esquire of Tamworth, Durham and Sandwich, New Hampshire*. Peterborough, N.H.: Richard R. Smith Co., Inc., 1963.

Harlow, Alvin F., *Steelways of New England*. New York: Creative Age Press, Inc., 1946.

Hitchcock, C. T., *The Geology of New Hampshire. Part I: Physical Geography*. Concord: Edward A. Jenks, State Printer, 1874.

Jewett, Sarah Orne, *Country By-Ways*. South Berwick, Maine: The Old Berwick Historical Society, 1981. Reprint of 1881 edition.

Mayo, Lawrence Shaw, *John Wentworth: Governor of New Hampshire 1767–1775*. Cambridge: Harvard University Press. 1921.

Merrit, Joseph F., *Tales of the North River*. Norwell, Mass.: n.p., n.d.

Parsons, Charles L., *The Capture of Fort William and Mary December 14 and 15, 1774*. n.p.: The William and Mary Committee of the New Hampshire American Revolution Bicentennial Commission, 1974. Reprint of 1906 article, with "Forward," by Joseph P. Copley.

Payson, Aurin M., and Laighton, Albert, compl., *The Poets of Portsmouth*. Boston: Walker, Wise and Co., 1865.

Pickett, Gertrude M., *Portsmouth's Heyday in Shipbuilding*.[Portsmouth]: Joseph G. Sawtelle, Publisher, 1979.

Raddall, Thomas H., *The Governor's Lady*. Garden City, N.Y.: Doubleday & Co., Inc., 1960.

Ricker, Jennie de R., *South Berwick: Pages from the Past*. n.p.; n.d.

Roberts, Kenneth. *Northwest Passage*. Garden City, N.Y.: Doubleday & Co., Inc., 1936.

——, *Rabble in Arms: A Chronicle of Arundel and the Burgoyne Invasion*. Garden City, N.Y.: Doubleday, Doran & Co., Inc., 1933.

Rowe, William Hutchinson, *The Maritime History of Maine*. New York: W. W. Norton & Co., 1948.

Saltonstall, William G., *Ports of Piscataqua*. Cambridge, Mass.: Harvard University Press, 1941.

Scales, John, *History of Dover, New Hampshire*. Manchester, N.H.: John B. Clarke Co., 1923.

——, *History of Strafford County, New Hampshire*. Chicago: Richmond-Arnold Publishing Co., 1914.

Seeger, Pete, *Folksinger*. New York: Simon and Schuster, 1972.

Squires, James Duane, *The Granite State of the United States: A History of New Hampshire from 1623 to the Present*. 3 vols. New York: The American Historical Company, Inc., 1956.

Stackpole, Everett S.; Thompson, Lucien; and Winthrop S. Meserve, *History of the Town of Durham*. Somersworth, N.H.:New Hampshire Publishing Co., 1973.

Thompson, Lawrance, and Winnick, R. H., *Robert Frost: The Later Years, 1938-1963*. New York: Holt, Rinehart and Winston, 1976.

Thompson, Mary P., *Landmarks in Ancient Dover, New Hampshire*. [Durham, N.H.]: Durham Historic Association, 1965.

Wadleigh, George, *Notable Events in the History of Dover*. Dover, N.H.: The Tufts College Press, 1913.

Webster's New Collegiate Dictionary. Springfield, Mass.: G. & C. Merriam Co., 1979.

Whittier, John Greenleaf, *The Complete Poetical Works of Whittier*. Cambridge, Mass.: Houghton Mifflin Co., 1892.

Wilcomb, Edgar Harlan, *Winnipesaukee Lake Country Gleanings*. Booklet E-1. Worcester, Mass.: n.p., 1923.

Wilcox, Philip A., *History in An Oystershell: A Brief History of Durham, New Hampshire 1600-1976*. Durham, N.H.: Durham Historic Association, 1976.

Works Progress Administration, *New Hampshire: A Guide to the Granite State*. Boston: Houghton Mifflin Co., 1938.

Unpublished Reports and Proceedings

Taylor, D. F[oster], "Survey #171,, The Piscataqua River Gundalow." Federal Project #6, Works Progress Administration, Wollaston, Mass.: Sponsored by the Smithsonian Institution of the U.S. National Museum, [1937]. 39 pages. (Typewritten.) Copies at the Portsmouth Athenaeum, Portsmouth, N.H., and at the Peabody Museum, Salem, Mass.

Public Documents

Boutin, Nathaniel, ed., *Collections of the New Hampshire Historical Society.* Concord: Published for the Society by G. Parker Lyon, 1863.

—— compl. and ed., *Provincial Papers: Documents and Records Relating to the Province of New-Hampshire From 1738 to 1749.* Nashua: Orren C. Moore, State Printer, 1871. Vol. VII.

Clark, William Bell, ed., *Naval Documents of the American Revolution.* Washington: Government Printing Office, 1966. Vol. II.

Hammond, Issac W., compl. and ed., *The State of New Hampshire Miscellaneous Provincial and State Papers 1629-1725.* Manchester: John B. Clarke, Public Printer, 1889, 1890. Vols. XVII-XVIII.

Hammond, Otis G., ed., *Letters and Papers of Major-General John Sullivan Continental Army.* Concord, N.H.: New Hampshire Historical Society, 1930. Vol. I (1771-1777).

Articles

Aykroyd, Elizabeth Rhoades, "Notes on the Raids on Fort William and Mary." *Historical New Hampshire* 32 (Fall 1977): 144-146.

Bowen, Roger, "The Saga of the Adams House." *Yankee* 31 (April 1967): 54-59, 108-110, 112-113.

Browne, Evelyn, "The Adamses of Adams Point." *New Hampshire Profiles* 10 (August 1961): 20-26, 40, 42.

Browne, George Waldo, "The Merrimack River: Boating Days and River Men." *Granite State Magazine* 1 (January-June 1906): 157-165.

Cole, Ichabod, "Notable Changes in the Navigation of the Piscataqua." *Old Eliot* 2 (May 1898): 73-75.

Day, Jane, "The Man Who Harvests Wooden Knees." *Yankee* 46 (April 1982): 172-175.

Georges, Justine Flint, "Captain Adams: The River Man—Who Never Retired." *Shoreliner* 1 (November 1950): 8-13.

Harvey, Joseph, "An Uncharted Town: Newmarket on the Lamprey—Historical Notes and Personal Sketches." *Granite Monthly* 40 (February and March 1908): 33-122.

Horgan, Tom, "Down East Cruise." *National Geographic* 102 (September 1952): 329-369.

Kaplan, Marion, "Twilight of the Arab Dhow." *National Geographic* 146 (September 1974): 330-351.

Klewin, Thomas E., "Gundalows on the Piscataqua." *New Hampshire Profiles* 22 (June 1973): 32-37.

Lovering, Frank W., "Salt Hay." *Yankee* 14 (August 1950): 40-41, 72.

Lovett, Robert W., "A Tidewater Merchant in New Hampshire." *The Business History Review* 33 (Spring 1959): 60-72. Reprinted as pamphlet.

Norris, Curtis B., "The Gundalow of Valcour Bay." *Yankee* 30 (September 1966): 160-165.

Ordway, Wallace B., "The Merrimac Gundalow and Gundalowmen." *American Neptune* 10 (October 1950): 249-263.

Page, Elwin L., "The King's Powder, 1774." *New England Quarterly* 18 (March 1945): 83-92.

Quackenbush, Julie, "Adams Point." *Catalyst* 4 (December 1978): 1-3.

Stevens, Lydia A., "Dover Landing from 1792 to 1842." *Granite Monthly* 39 (May 1907): 150-156.

Sweet, Douglas H., "New Hampshire on the Road to Revolution: Fort William and Mary, A Decisive Step." *Historical New Hampshire* 29 (Winter 1974): 229-256.

Taylor, D. Foster, "The Gundalow *Fanny M.*" *American Neptune* 2 (July 1942): 209-222.

———, "The Piscataqua River Gundalow." *American Neptune* 2 (April 1942): 127-139.

Wilderson, Paul W. III, "John Wentworth's Narrative of the Raids on Fort William and Mary." *Historical New Hampshire* 32 (Winter 1977): 228-236.

———, "The Raids on Fort William and Mary: Some New Evidence." *Historical New Hampshire* 30 (Fall 1975): 178-202.

Newspapers

Durham Chronicle, 15 May 1732, special supplement of *Foster's Daily Democrat*, 12 May 1982.

Foster's Daily Democrat (Dover, N.H.).

Hampton Union (Hampton, N.H.).

Manchester Union-Leader.

National Fisherman (Camden, Maine).

New Hampshire Times (Concord, N.H.).

New York Times.

Piscataqua Current (Portsmouth, N.H.).

Portsmouth Herald.

Soundings (Essex, Connecticut).

Transcript (Dover, N.H.).

York County Coast Star (Kennebunk, Maine).

Manuscript Collections

Adams, Adams Family Papers, Dimond Library, University of New Hampshire, Durham, New Hampshire.

Chase, Chase Family Papers, Strawbery Banke Library, Portsmouth, New Hampshire.

Frost, Joseph W. P., "Gundalows," Portsmouth Athenaeum Library, Portsmouth, New Hampshire. Eight page typescript.

Kittery Historical and Naval Museum, Papers, Kittery Historical and Naval Museum, Kittery, Maine.

Petitions and Province Records, Department of State, Division of Records
    Management and Archives, Concord, New Hampshire.
Piscataqua Gundalow Project Papers, Marine Program Building, University of
    New Hampshire, Durham, New Hampshire.
Saltonstall, William G., Marion, Mass. One Letter to R. E. Winslow. In posses-
    sion of the author, Rye, New Hampshire.
State of New Hampshire, Certificate, Bureau of Vital Records & Health
    Statistics, Concord, New Hampshire.
Whitehouse, Robert, Collection. Note cards, photocopies, drawings, "Gundalows,"
    Fourteen page typescript, and other gundalow materials, Rollinsford, New
    Hampshire.

Interviews

Armitage, Peggy. Portsmouth, New Hampshire, 8 March 1982.
Brake, Stephen. Portsmouth, New Hampshire, 21 May 1982.
Browne, Evelyn. Durham, New Hampshire, 15 January 1982.
Clark, Charles E. Durham, New Hampshire, 15 January 1982.
Corell, Robert W. Durham, New Hampshire, 1 March 1982.
Dennett, William E. Kittery, Maine, 26 December 1981.
Dudley, Thomas W. Portsmouth, New Hampshire, 29 January 1982
Eger, Robert. Portsmouth, New Hampshire, 5 May, 1982
Gallant, Richard. Portsmouth, New Hampshire, 19 February 1982.
Gebow, David. Portsmouth, New Hampshire, 21 May 1982.
Happny, Peter. Portsmouth, New Hampshire, 25 January 1982.
Hayes, Barry. Portsmouth, New Hampshire, 21 May 1982.
Hickey, Albert E. Portsmouth, New Hampshire, 8 March 1982.
Jalbert, Edward. Portsmouth, New Hampshire, 17 April 1982.
Johnson, Philip. East Lebanon, Maine, 9 February 1982.
McIntosh, David C. "Bud." Dover, New Hampshire, 17 February 1982.
McIntosh, Edward "Ned." Dover, New Hampshire, 12 May 1982.
Meeker, Sharon. Durham, New Hampshire, 29 June 1982.
Roberts, Lewis, Jr. Durham, New Hampshire, 8 February 1982.
Sawyer, Warren. Newmarket, New Hampshire, 5 February 1982.
Stivers, Irene. Greenland, New Hampshire, 19 May 1982.
Vaughn, Charles. Portsmouth, New Hampshire, 29 January 1982.
Whitehouse, Robert A. South Berwick, Maine, 7 January 1982.

Dates are given only for initial interviews. In many instances, these interviews
led to additional conversations and correspondence.

Symbols used in captions for sources of photographs

DAC   Douglas Armsden Collection, Kittery Point, Maine.

EHS   Exeter Historical Society, Exeter, New Hampshire.

GB   *Great Bay: A Visual History*, UNH Publication, (1970).

HU   *Hampton Union*, Hampton, New Hampshire.

HUP   Harvard University Press, Cambridge, Massachusetts.

NHA   New Hampshire Archives, Concord, New Hampshire.

NHS   Newmarket Historical Society, Newmarket, New Hampshire.

NHSH   New Hampshire State House, Concord, New Hampshire.

NHT   *New Hampshire Times*, Concord, New Hampshire.

PA   Portsmouth Athenaeum, Portsmouth, New Hampshire.

PGP   Piscataqua Gundalow Project.

PM   Peabody Museum, Salem, Massachusetts.

RWC   Robert Whitehouse Collection, Rollinsford, New Hampshire.

SHS   Seabrook Historical Society, Seabrook, New Hampshire.

SPNEA   Society for the Preservation of New England Antiquities, Boston, Massachusetts.

UNHD   University of New Hampshire Docent Program, Durham, New Hampshire.

UNHMS   University of New Hampshire Media Services Department, Dimond Library, Durham, New Hampshire.

Index

About the Author

Richard Elliott Winslow III was born in Boston, Massachusetts, in 1934 and has lived in New Hampshire periodically since 1938. A resident of Portsmouth since 1957, he recieved his Master's degree in History from the University of New Hampshire in 1965. After obtaining his doctorate, he has taught, edited and written in the field of American History. He is now a free-lance writer and a librarian.

Winslow is the author of *General John Sedgwick: The Story of a Union Corps Commander* (1982), and the associate editor of *The Cormany Diaries: A Northern Family in the Civil War* (also 1982).

An avid outdoorsman who enjoys hiking, canoeing, and whitewater rafting, Winslow canoed the Allagash River in northern Maine during the summer of 1974. The sense of freedom and independence he found on that river and on other canoeing and rafting trips has enriched his understanding of the gundalow captains on the Piscataqua, who appear in this book.